SEMINAR STUDIES IN HISTORY
General Editor: Roger Lockyer

English Catholicism 1558–1642: Continuity and Change

Alan Dures

LONGMAN GROUP UK LIMITED
*Longman House, Burnt Mill, Harlow, Essex CM20 2JE, England
and Associated Companies throughout the World.*

First published 1983
Third impression 1988
ISBN 0 582 35229 0

Set in 10/11 Baskerville, Linotron 202

*Produced by Longman Singapore Publishers Pte Ltd
Printed in Singapore*

Contents

Acknowledgements

We are grateful to Longman Group Ltd and the author, Rev. Philip Caraman for permission to reproduce an extract from *William Weston*.

Cover: A satirical print of Jesuits at Council In England. Fotomas Index, London.

Seminar Studies in History
Founding Editor: Patrick Richardson

Introduction

The Seminar Studies series was conceived by Patrick Richardson, whose experience of teaching history persuaded him of the need for something more substantial than a textbook chapter but less formidable than the specialised full-length academic work. He was also convinced that such studies, although limited in length, should provide an up-to-date and authoritative introduction to the topic under discussion as well as a selection of relevant documents and a comprehensive bibliography.

Patrick Richardson died in 1979, but by that time the Seminar Studies series was firmly established, and it continues to fulfil the role he intended for it. This book, like others in the series, is therefore a living tribute to a gifted and original teacher.

Note on the System of References:
A bold number in round brackets (**5**) in the text refers the reader to the corresponding entry in the Bibliography section at the end of the book. A bold number in square brackets, preceded by 'doc' [**docs 6, 8**] refers the reader to the corresponding items in the section of Documents, which follows the main text.

ROGER LOCKYER
General Editor

Preface

I am much indebted to a number of people in the writing of this book. The late Patrick Richardson, founder editor of the series and former colleague, encouraged me to contribute to it, while the late Professor Hurstfield first stirred my interest in English Catholicism in the Tudor and Stuart period. While writing the book I have received considerable help from Dr Alan Davidson, Dr Christopher Haigh and Professor John Bossy, all of whom read the manuscript and made many helpful suggestions. My debt to these last two scholars will be apparent to all who read the book. In this respect, I am particularly grateful to Dr Haigh for allowing me to read and to use extensively two pre-publication articles. I am also grateful to Roger Lockyer, new editor of the series, for his assistance in the final preparation of the manuscript.

My greatest debt is to my wife for her practical help and constant encouragement.

Alan Dures

vi

Foreword

The preamble to the *Act in Restraint of Appeals* of 1533 which declares that 'This realm of England is an Empire' serves to emphasise that the changes in English history from 1533 to 1536, when centuries of allegiance to Rome were reversed, were more of a political and legal revolution than a religious one. The Reformation was a central element in the development of the English national state. 'The subjection of the Church', writes Professor Elton, 'formed the most striking but not the sole manifestation of a general policy designed to create the unitary realm of England under the legislative sovereignty of the King in Parliament.' (**34**). The Reformation was prompted and accompanied by changes in religious doctrine and popular religious culture, but such developments are less easily gauged than the religious policies of the Crown.

These policies were far from clearcut as long as Henry VIII lived, but from 1547 the Government gave a lead to protestantism. The First Edwardian Prayer Book of 1549 was ambiguous enough on such central issues as the eucharist to be capable of both a protestant and catholic interpretation, but only because Parliament had toned down Cranmer's original version which denied transubstantiation and abolished the mass. The 1552 Prayer Book, however, was unambiguously protestant; it marked the arrival of the protestant Reformation in England.

One of the main problems in analysing religious attitudes in Tudor England is to identify sources and criteria which indicate popular beliefs rather than mere conformity to government policy. Dr Palliser, in an article in a recent book (**43**), discussed a range of evidence which might help in judging religious beliefs in particular areas, and these include rebellions with religious overtones, the extent of clerical marriage, doctrinal beliefs as expressed in wills, and the numer of Marian exiles in a region. The picture that emerges from the use of such criteria confirms the traditional distinction between the more protestant south-east and the conservative north and west. As early as 1537, the will of Alderman Monmouth of London testifies clearly to the protestant belief in salvation 'solely through the merits of Christ's passion'. Clerical marriage was legal-ised in 1549, but some of the Suffolk clergy had married as early as 1536–37. By 1553 nearly one-third of the London clergy and a quarter of the clergy in Suffolk, Norfolk and Essex were married. Of 360 protestants who went into exile in Mary's reign, whose place of origin can be identified, some two-fifths came from the south-east of England. Townsmen in the south-east readily accepted protestantism, which was firmly established in Colchester and Ipswich by 1553 (**43**).

By contrast, Yorkshire and Lancashire had few married clergy and a relatively small number of Marian exiles. Dr Haigh has shown that there was great resistance to the Reformation in Lan-cashire, and he concludes that 'the fairly intensive efforts at conver-sion made in the reign of Edward had reaped only a meagre har-vest and protestantism had gained very little support by 1559' (**40** p. 225). The north remained generally conservative, despite pock-ets of protestantism in the textile areas of Lancashire and the West Riding. The absence of serious rebellion in the north in 1549 was probably due to the memory of the savage repression of the Pil-grimage of Grace (1536) and loyalty to the Tudors rather than to support for the Edwardian Reformation. In 1550 a priest was of the opinion that the region 'from Trent northward' was slower than the south in abolishing catholic ritual.

However, some qualifications need to be made to the traditional pattern discussed so far. Professor Dickens has shown that within conservative Yorkshire there was a popular protestantism, though he stressed that it was difficult to quantify (**31**). In the west coun-try in 1548 Thomas Hancock found a group at Poole in Dorset 'that were the first that in that part of England were called protes-tant'. Some communities were split religiously. Early in Mary's reign a catholic preacher in Bristol said that 'Here among you in this city some will hear mass, some will hear none…some will pray for the dead, some will not. I hear of much dissension among you.' (**43**, p. 47)

Such evidence makes it extremely difficult to generalise about the state of religious beliefs in England in 1553. Professor Elton has re-cently argued that the Edwardian Reformation established its effec-tiveness and that 'by 1553 England was almost certainly nearer to being a protestant country than to anything else' (**34**). Even if such a judgement is accepted, the Marian reaction appears to have been successful in achieving conformity, though little was done to renew the spiritual basis of catholicism. In Suffolk and Kent, for example, where the Edwardian Reformation was influential, the conservative reaction in Mary's reign was still significant. The effectiveness of the Marian reaction suggests that protestantism had not developed very deep roots. From the 1530s until 1558 a number of areas showed strong allegiance to traditional forms of religion; in 1551 the Government picked out Devon, Hampshire, Lancashire, Yorkshire, Wales and the Scottish Borders as being particularly hostile to protestantism. In 1558, therefore, conservative religion was still powerful in many counties and this survival formed the basis of early Elizabethan catholicism.

Alan Dures

Part One: The Background

1 The Years of Survival

On 28 November 1558 Elizabeth I entered the city of London. Her welcome was somewhat muted and her entry had to be carefully managed to give the impression of popular enthusiasm. But the broadsheets of 1558 and 1559 suggest that many protestant zealots saw Elizabeth as their saviour. This, too, was the role assigned to her in Foxe's *Acts and Monuments* published in 1563, while the news of Elizabeth's accession had brought the protestant émigrés flocking home. The new Queen never fulfilled the extravagant hopes of the English protestants, but it seems possible that in November 1558 she was already committed to a reversal of her sister's religious policy. However, Elizabeth proceeded with caution, acting perhaps on the advice of her loyal follower Sir Nicholas Throgmorton, to 'succeed happily through a discreet beginning' (**57**, vol. I, p. 35). She retained among her councillors the moderate Nicholas Heath, Archbishop of York and Mary's former Chancellor, and it may well be that Heath's last attendance at the Privy Council, on 5 January 1559, marks the point at which Elizabeth decided to inform the council of her intention to break with Rome.

When Parliament met in January 1559 its main function was formally to re-establish Elizabeth's control over the English church. The hitherto accepted view of the evolution of the Elizabethan settlement, put forward by Sir John Neale (**57**, vol. I, pp. 51–84), assumes that the government originally intended that Parliament should merely assent to the Queen's Supremacy, for a provision attached to the Supremacy bill, which was introduced on 9 February 1559, to allow communion in both kinds, suggests that at this stage the Government did not envisage a separate Act of Uniformity (**29**). This interim settlement would have been little in advance of the arrangements in the reign of Henry VIII; but, to a man, the spiritual lords refused to support the bill. On 24 March 1559, when MPs were expecting the Supremacy bill to become law and Parliament to be dissolved, Elizabeth prorogued Parliament until after Easter. On Parliament's recall, an Act of Uniformity was passed as well as that of Supremacy. According to Neale's interpretation, Elizabeth changed her mind and decided to bring in the Uniformity bill as a result of protestant pressure in the House of Commons (**57**).

This interpretation has recently been challenged by Professor Elton, following the researches of Mr N. J. Jones. Elton argues that 'the Settlement emerged virtually in the shape designed beforehand by the Queen and the council . . . there was no effective forcing of the pace by zealous protestants in the Commons' (**102**, p. 272). The government had not introduced the Uniformity bill earlier because of the need firstly to reduce the opposition in the House of Lords and also because Elizabeth probably wanted to proceed by gradual stages [**doc. 1**]. Moreover Parliament was recalled after Easter not primarily to pass the Act of Uniformity, but to ensure that the prickly problem of restoring certain lands, taken by the Marian bishops, to their lay owners, should be resolved (**102**).

The final Elizabethan church settlement was a compromise, but one which may have been shaped as much by the conservative opposition in the Lords as by protestant pressure in the Commons. The Act of Supremacy gave Elizabeth the title of Supreme Governor and not her father's title of Supreme Head. Edwin Sandys thought that the Queen was satisfying protestant criticism of royal supremacy, but it is more likely that she was trying to conciliate her catholic subjects, especially in view of the episcopal opposition in the Lords. The Act of Uniformity was based mainly on the protestant Second Edwardian Prayer Book, but with two important qualifications. The ornaments rubric stipulated that the use of vestments and ornaments should be the same as in 1548, while the formula for the eucharist made it possible to believe in the real presence. These conservative provisions may have been necessary to get the Uniformity bill through the Lords; even so, eighteen lay peers as well as the bishops registered their opposition. This hybrid settlement had its political uses. When the French ambassador visited Archbishop Parker at Canterbury in 1564, Parker was careful to explain the similarities to catholicism of the newly established church, which still preserved days of abstinence and had music in its service. The French ambassador was duly impressed and conceded that the English 'were in religion very nigh to them' (**39**).

The Marian bishops nevertheless rejected the settlement. Cuthbert Tunstall, Bishop of Durham, spoke for all of them when he protested to Cecil that he could not consent 'to have any new doctrine taught in my diocese'. The parochial clergy did not, however, follow the lead of their superiors, though the generally accepted figure of only 300 resignations out of 8,000 incumbents is probably too low. There is plenty of evidence that a number of clergy who stayed on still adhered to the old faith [**doc. 2**] but their readiness to conform contrasts sharply with the refusal of the catholic bishops. The reaction of the laity to the Elizabethan settlement is much more difficult to assess. The settlement was received differently from county to county. Nicholas Sander, who was later to become a catholic exile at Louvain, wrote in 1561 that 'the most distant parts of the kingdom are most averse to heresy'. Protestantism, claimed Sander, was restricted to the towns, so that 'not so many as one in a hundred of the English are protestant'. In London the abolition of catholic worship was carried out with a zeal bordering on vandalism; stained glass windows were broken and statues destroyed 'as if it had beene the sacking of some hostile city'. (**55**, p. 32). Moreover there was also a great deal of apathy and confusion; John Jewel lamented that 'many will believe neither side, whatsoever they allege . . . so hardened their hearts' (**44**, p. 58).

It is not simply the lack of detailed evidence which makes it impossible to give accurate estimates of catholic strength in 1559. The very definition of catholicism is difficult, for it covers a wide spectrum of opinion. Various strands of catholicism can be identified. There were, for instance, those who adhered to medieval catholic rituals and rites out of a sense of deep conservatism. Secondly, there were those whose adherence to the old faith was more articulate, perhaps under the influence of catholic literature from the continent, or of the Marian priests, but who nevertheless attended the Anglican church. These were known as Church Papists. Thirdly, there were the 'recusants' – a term applied to catholics who refused to attend Anglican services and also to those catholics who refused the Oath of Supremacy out of a belief in papal supremacy. There is little evidence of strong support for papal leadership, which is hardly surprising, as England had been in schism since 1534, except for Mary's brief reign. But if we use 'catholic' in its widest sense, we find plenty of evidence of strong survival, especially in certain parts of the country.

In the 1560s Yorkshire showed a deep religious conservatism. The visitation of Archbishop Thomas Young of York in 1567–68 found that in Holderness, in the East Riding of Yorkshire, several parish priests continued the catholic practice of masses for the dead, while in some parishes images were still worshipped and the pulpit was 'undecentlie kept'. A blatant example of catholic survival was in the parish of Swine, where the old badge of the Pilgrimage of Grace was displayed. The visitation records a complaint of 'a cross of woode standinge over the north ile with a scutcheon having the figure of the v woondes and other superstitious thinges therein' (**82**, p. 161). At Ripon in 1567 three priests were operating a mass centre in the church's 'Lady Loft'. This had been crammed with images and the priests offered masses to rival the official services in the chancel. Despite the strong evidence of catholicism surviving in Yorkshire in the 1560s there are few indications of recusancy. But by the 1570s there are signs in some areas of the beginnings of catholic withdrawal from services at the parish church. At a parish near York in the mid 1570s few, if any, turned up for the services, and the minister regularly locked up the church when none responded to the call of the bell (**105**). By 1570–72 the basis for later recusancy was already being laid in the parish of Masham. Deprived Marian priests stayed with local people, hosts were made for use in masses, and the protestant curate was ill-treated by conservative parishioners (**105**, p 44).

Catholicism was also strong in Lancashire. Strype, in his *Annals of the Reformation*, complained that 'mass [was] commonly said, priests harboured, the Book of Common Prayer and the service of the Church established by law laid aside'. Catholicism flourished in Lancashire partly because the Anglican church was so weak and poorly endowed. Bishop Downham complained in 1568 that in the Diocese of Chester (which included the county of Lancashire) he possessed 'the least revenue that any man of my calling have in this realm' (**40**, p 225). Recusant priests – that is Marian priests who had been deprived of office or who had resigned after 1559 – made a greater contribution to the maintenance of catholicism in Lancashire than seems likely in most other counties. In the first decade of the reign there were some forty recusant priests in four deaneries of southern Lancashire, whereas the Established Church clergy numbered no more than seventy-nine. Moreover, as the visitation of 1571 alarmingly pointed out, many of the Established Church clergy were strongly sympathetic to catholicism and gave support to recusant priests. Nicholas Daniel, the puritan vicar of Preston, complained of William Wall, a curate who had formally conformed, yet who continued the catholic practice of giving the 'sacrament into the mouths' since the parishioners objected to taking it into their hands. The same William Wall also condoned the practice of catholics having their children baptised at home by recusant priests, rather than in the parish church (**86**). Despite such catholicism, there was little recusancy in Lancashire in the 1560s.

Only eight recusants, mainly leading gentry, were called before a special ecclesiastical commission in 1568, though this was probably an understatement of Lancashire recusancy. Most Lancashire catholics conformed to the new religious settlement to some degree and William Allen admitted that 'many laymen who believed the faith in their hearts and heard mass when they could, frequented the schismatic church' (**86**).

Durham showed considerable sympathy with the old faith and conservatism was reinforced by a supply of refugee Scottish priests. In 1560 the Duke of Norfolk found altars still standing in churches, while in 1564 the clergy and churchwardens of Seaton were imprisoned for keeping 'monuments of superstition and idolatry' and for celebrating catholic rites. In 1571 Thomas Wright, an Established Church cleric, was deprived for saying 'Mattins of the Virgin Mary'. Yet despite evidence of considerable catholic strength, the only detected case of recusancy was that of Elizabeth, wife of Richard Branding, who was presented at Jarrow in 1565 (**85**). Characteristic of catholicism in Durham in the 1560s was the bastard-feudal connection of the Nevilles, the most powerful lay landlords in the county. Henry, fifth Earl of Westmorland, had been a staunch supporter of the Marian regime. His son Charles, who became the sixth Earl in 1563, maintained two catholic chaplains, one of whom, Robert Preston, played a leading role in the rebellion of 1569. Gentry such as the Trollopps of Thornley also kept catholic chaplains. In the revolt of the Northern Earls, many of the clergy of the Established Church assisted in the destruction of protestant service books and church furniture (**85**).

Sander's generalisation that catholicism was strongest in the remoter areas seems therefore well founded. The diocese of Hereford on the Welsh borders returned the highest number of Justices of the Peace who in 1564 were 'unfavourable' to the Anglican settlement, and the Welsh dioceses showed similar conservative tendencies to those of the north [**doc. 2**]. The early survival of catholicism certainly owed a great deal to social and geographical factors. Much depended on the conservatism and inaccessibility of the remoter areas of the country. But there were also catholic strongholds outside these areas. West Sussex, for instance, showed a strong inclination towards catholicism, despite the general protestant sympathies of the southern and south-eastern counties. It has been estimated that among the leading gentry and aristocratic families in Sussex, catholics outnumbered protestants by almost two to one in the 1560s (**52**, p. 259). Moreover, the catholic peers, the twelfth

Earl of Arundel and his son-in-law Lord Lumley, were Lord-Lieutenants of the county until 1569, when their close connection with the rebel Northern Earls made their dismissal imperative. Catholic influence continued after that date, however, as Lord Montague, who subsequently became a leading recusant, was in the lieutenancy as late as 1585 (**52**). There were, in fact, pockets of catholicism in every county. A census of nonconformity in Suffolk in the early 1560s lists 128 names, many of them catholic. In 1561 Robert Horn, the recently appointed Bishop of Winchester, complained to William Cecil of the number of people in Hampshire who were resisting the new religion.

The 1564 episcopal reports to the Privy Council on the religious affiliations of the Justices of the Peace provide a rough guide to the strength of the old faith among upper gentry families. The reports must be used with caution. The bishops classified the justices into those who were 'favourable', 'unfavourable' or 'neutral' towards the Elizabethan settlement. Such categories are vague and subjective, and some bishops sent out more detailed reports than others. Nevertheless, even after all these reservations, the 1564 returns show a strong religious conservatism among the office-holders. Just under a third of the justices were described as 'unfavourable' to the religious settlement (**66**, p. 26). Moreover, as Hassell Smith has shown (**62**), the Commissions of the Peace had already been remodelled in order to reduce the catholic element among the justices. The percentage of religious conservatives on the Commissions of the Peace in 1564 probably reflects the cautious policy of the Elizabethan government. It is also a comment on the level of conformity, including the taking of the Oath of Supremacy, among those who were still inclined to the old faith. After the outbreak of the Northern Rebellion, all office-holders were tendered the Oath of Uniformity also, and known catholics in almost every county signed the Oath.

The outstanding characteristic of Elizabethan catholicism in the first twenty years of the reign was its partly conformist nature (**76**). One of the most obstinate recusants in Northamptonshire in the 1580s, Robert Price, had previously conformed for many years. When asked in 1582 how long it was since he had attended an Anglican church, he told the court that 'he hath not come to church this twelve months past...yet he confesseth that he did come to church for the space of ten years last before that, and received the communion at sundry times' (**3**). Lord Montague of Cowdray in Sussex is a better known example. Sir Anthony

Browne, Lord Montague's father, had been a Henrician catholic and the family were outstanding catholics up to the Civil War. Yet Lord Montague made at least an occasional attendance at Anglican services even into the 1580s, possibly to maintain his position as Lord-Lieutenant of the county. Reproached by his new chaplain, Father Robert Gray, Montague fell on his knees and 'humbly admitted himself to the censure and piously promised never thenceforward to be present at heretical service'. This was probably in the late 1580s and thereafter he became a thoroughgoing recusant, though his peerage and court influence prevented him from suffering the usual penalties (**52**, pp. 221, 231).

Within its conformist nature there were nevertheless different strands of catholic survival. Yorkshire in the 1560s shows a strong adherence to medieval ritual, while Lancashire had early connections with continental catholicism through Allen and Vaux. But medievalism disappeared as the clergy were brought under stricter control by the government, so catholic practices could be continued only within the safety of aristocratic and gentry households or in areas of lax administration. There was an affinity between the more conservative classes and the old faith. Adherence to catholicism did not necessarily entail a deep theological commitment; it could also stem from support for a social order which, it was felt, was being undermined by protestantism. On one level, protestantism was disliked because it was a religion of 'basket makers and beer brewers' (**76**). Catholicism was the 'natural' religion, protestantism a dangerous innovation [**doc. 6**]. The more conservative aristocracy and gentry, especially in the more feudal conditions of the northern counties, felt that both the Henrician and Elizabethan Reformations were an unwarranted intrusion into their 'estate'. But such attitudes did not necessarily mean absence from their parish church, as many had proprietary interests in their local churches. The close connection between the gentry and the parish church can be seen in the will of Jasper Leeke, a catholic from Edmonton, Middlesex, who in 1570 left a pair of gold candlesticks to the parish church 'should the masse ever be said there again'. The nature of the catholic survival, with its considerable dependence on the scattered households of the gentry and the aristocracy, did much to ensure that no national catholic leadership emerged (**76**).

In addition to this 'seigneurial' catholicism, however, there was also a peasant catholicism. Dr Haigh has argued forcefully that the gentry domination of English catholicism was not inevitable, but rather the result of a deliberate policy by the missionary priests

(**106**). Certainly the absence of a centralised and centrally financed ecclesiastical organisation made seventeenth-century catholicism very dependent on gentry resources, but in the Elizabethan period there was a vigorous catholic survival outside the gentry households, especially in the remoter parts of Durham, Yorkshire and Lancashire. Ripon, as we have already seen, was in trouble for retaining conservative religious practices in the 1560s; it continued to show hostility to the Established Church in the 1570s and by 1604 recorded 120 papists. Yet there was no substantial gentry leadership and its flourishing catholicism was due more to adminstrative isolation (**105**, pp. 44–5). Even in the less remote areas of the south, peasant catholicism was evident in the late Elizabethan period. About 1590 the Jesuit Thomas Stanney was requested to go round the Hampshire villages to minister to the poor. When he showed signs of reluctance, he was told by his guide that 'we still have a great many hungry souls that want bread, and there is no-one to give it to them; we have many also that would be glad to shake off the yoke of bondage, heresy, and embrace the Catholic faith, and I can find none to help them and receive them into the Church' (**106**, p 143).

The lack of catholic leadership, the relatively weak links with continental catholicism and the conservatism of many of its supporters, might in themselves be sufficient to explain why adherence to the old faith was not translated into more positive opposition to the religious settlement of 1559. There were, however, other contributory factors. Outstanding among these are Elizabethan policy towards the catholics in the first twenty years of the reign and the total absence of papal leadership for the English catholics in the 1560s (**55**).

Elizabethan policy

English historians have tended to describe Elizabeth's policy as very lenient in the early years of the reign (**60**). The Marian bishops avoided the death penalty and some even enjoyed a degree of liberty, depending mainly on English foreign policy. The catholic laity suffered relatively mild penalties under the Acts of Supremacy and Uniformity. Failure to attend church resulted in a 12d. fine, while refusal of the Oath of Supremacy meant loss of office. Anyone who wrote or spoke in favour of papal supremacy suffered loss of goods for his first offence, *praemunire* (forfeiture of all goods and imprisonment) for the second and the death penalty for the third. The parliamentary legislation of 1563, however, provided for harsher measures. Subscription to the Oath of Supremacy was required from a greatly enlarged number of clerical and lay officials, including schoolmasters, lawyers, court officials and MPs. The nobility, however, were exempt. For the rest of society the penalty for refusing the Oath of Supremacy for a second time was death. Any priest guilty of saying mass, or any layman who 'procured mass to be said or willingly suffered it to be said', was liable to the death penalty (**57**, vol. 1, pp. 116–20). The lesser penalty of a 100 mark fine was levied on those who merely attended the mass. Such measures reflected the anti-catholic feeling of Parliament, especially of the House of Commons, and were not indicative of government policy. Elizabeth ensured that no one suffered the death penalty through refusing the Oath of Surpemacy, since she instructed Archbishop Parker not to offer it twice. Nor did anyone suffer the death penalty for saying mass before 1577, though the 100 mark fine was exacted from some people for attending mass.

The 1563 Parliament provided a forum for debate on Elizabethan policy towards catholics since 1559. The catholic Lord Montague argued that harsher measures were unnecessary, since the catholics disturbed neither the spiritual nor the temporal wellbeing of the realm (**57**, vol. 1, p. 120). However, Dean Nowell of St Paul's, in his opening address to Parliament, criticised Elizabethan policy and called for the death penalty for the upholders of false religion; heresy had to be 'cut off' before it infected the rest of christian society [**doc. 3**]. Elizabeth, however, refused to heed Nowell's advice. The evidence of the 1564 episcopal reports on the JPs and the extent of catholic office-holding in counties such as Sussex, suggests strongly that catholics were not even dismissed from office in the 1560s if they took the Oath of Supremacy. But perhaps Elizabeth's policy towards catholics is better described as cautious rather than lenient. Her first aim was to encourage all her subjects to conform to the religious settlement. She could best achieve this by contenting herself with a token conformity from her catholic subjects in the hope that time and pressure would effect a total conversion. In the North Riding of Yorkshire some 75 per cent of the leading families were catholic (**28**). In such an area any policy based on swift rather than slow conversion would have required draconian measures which could not have been enforced. Persecution on a large scale, involving loss of life and property, would have been extremely disruptive. As the Jesuit William Weston was to observe later, 'it is impossible for such a violent disturbance of property not to bring with it a great disorder in all parts and the imminent ruin of the whole country'.

The leniency of the Elizabethan government in the 1560s was in some cases due to its inability to carry out a more vigorous policy. Elizabeth and Cecil were highly dissatisfied with the state of religion in Lancashire. Cecil received numerous gloomy reports on the county, and Elizabeth expressed her dissatisfaction with Bishop Downham by appointing the Bishop of Carlisle to hold a visitation of Lancashire in 1570. But there was little more the government could do without taking the kind of drastic action which would have been politically dangerous. Both Downham and the Earl of Derby, Lord-Lieutenant of the county, were popular figures in Lancashire among the catholic gentry, and it is perhaps due to their leniency that there were no moves in Lancashire in 1569 to support the Rebellion of the Northern Earls.

Where government possessed the necessary power it struck out against overt catholic activities and recusancy. In London, as early as 1560, English catholics attending mass on the Feast of the Purification were arrested at the French Embassy. In 1563 the government forbade foreign catholics who were not members of diplomatic missions to attend mass at the embassy chapels. Numerous catholics were imprisoned for breaking the new religious laws. Sir Thomas Stradling of Glamorgan was put in the Tower for allegedly carving a cross on a tree which had blown down in a storm on his estate. Six Oxford University students who resisted the removal of the crucifix from their chapel were imprisoned in 1560. A Marian priest, Nicholas Bush, was sent to the Fleet prison for administering the sacraments according to the catholic rites to Lady Hobblethorne of Essex (**66**, p. 20). In 1565 a number of Yorkshire catholics were imprisoned. Sir Thomas Metham was the most unyielding. He refused to attend Anglican services or to read religious books other than those approved by the catholic church.

As relations between Spain and England deteriorated in 1568, the year which also saw the flight to England of the catholic Mary Queen of Scots, the government made greater efforts to achieve conformity within the Established Church. The Justices of the Peace were instructed to support the evangelising efforts of the Anglican clergy, and a number of prominent catholics were arrested in 1568, including two women of high social rank, Lady Brown and Lady Cary, for having mass celebrated in their houses. The government's actions showed an intensification of its policy since 1559. It now aimed to secure the conformity of the leading catholics in every county community. If this failed, the most prominent recusants were segregated from the community by imprisonment or by some restrictions on their freedom in order to neutralise their influence (**66**).

One of the factors which prevented a more positive catholic rejection of the Elizabethan church and a speedier withdrawal from parochial life into recusancy, was the lack of papal leadership. It was not until 1562 that the Vatican made an authoritative statement prohibiting catholics from attending Anglican services, and this was only in response to an enquiry by certain English catholics. Even then the papacy took no steps to publicise its prohibition widely until 1566, when Lawrence Vaux attempted to make the papal decree known in Lancashire and other counties. Given the poor relations between England and Rome, even in Mary's reign, any papal attempts to impose recusancy as a catholic norm in the 1560s, when many parish churches were still ineffectively protestantised, might have been a failure. But the papacy could have done more to endorse the lead given by the catholic bishops in 1559.

Elizabeth might have been forced into a more vigorous policy if the papacy had taken a positive attitude towards English catholicism. But papal policy in the early 1560s was based on the assumption, encouraged by Philip II of Spain, that England could be won back to catholicism by diplomacy. Initially, Pope Pius IV hoped that England would attend the Council of Trent. Elizabeth seems to have been enthusiastic, and that good protestant Nicholas Throgmorton told the Venetian ambassador that the Queen would send representatives if the Council were 'free'. But in December 1560 the Pope asserted his ultimate control over the Council, which meant that it would no longer be 'free' as Elizabeth understood the term. From this point, England was probably not seriously interested in attending the Council of Trent, but the papacy continued to press Elizabeth to receive its nuncio Martinengo. De Quadra, the Spanish ambassador, worked assiduously for better Anglo-papal relations and it was a bitter blow when the Privy Council refused entry to Martinengo in May 1561. Despite this rebuff to papal diplomacy, it was not until 1563 that Pope Pius became convinced that England could only be retained in the catholic church by political and military means. This view was shared by catholic exiles at Louvain and in June 1563 some of these exiles requested that the Council of Trent should declare Elizabeth excommunicate. But Spain and the Empire were horrified, as both be-

11

lieved that this would increase their own religious difficulties in Germany and the Netherlands. Under pressure from the Habsburgs, therefore, Pius IV dropped the idea of excommunicating Elizabeth (**45, 39**).

The negotiations between England and Rome in the early 1560s sustained catholic hopes that Elizabeth might reverse the 1559 settlement. In May 1561 Cecil complained that the negotiations had raised catholic expectations which he now thought 'necessary to dull'. Elizabeth, however, may have been happy to encourage catholics in this way. By 1565 papal policy towards England was hardening. Pius openly declared that military intervention was probably the only answer to the problem of heresy in England and Scotland. Moreover papal policy now met with a positive response in Spain. Philip II was drawing closer to the Guises, the extreme catholic faction in France, and was therefore more sympathetic to the claims of Mary Queen of Scots to the English succession. In October 1565 he declared in a letter that 'when the time comes to throw off the mask and bestir ourselves . . . the Pope and I will consider the manner in which we may aid and promote that cause of God which now the Queen of Scotland upholds, since it is manifest that she is the gate by which religion must enter the realm of England, all others being now closed' (**39**, p. 308).

Anglo-papal relations worsened as the 1560s progressed. In 1566 the new Pope, Pius V, made conciliatory gestures to Elizabeth, but soon became convinced that the English Queen could only be forced into obedience. Philip II was too preoccupied with the problems of the Turks and the Netherlands to consider seriously taking military action. But the isolation of England was growing. In the winter of 1567–68 the Earl of Sussex reported that there was no possibility of a marriage between Elizabeth and the catholic Archduke Charles of Austria. By the spring of 1568 Mary Stuart had been expelled from Scotland and was in Cumberland. Before the year was out, William Cecil had seized Philip II's bullion ships, the final move in the breaking of friendship with Spain. Soon the Elizabethan government would be faced with its most serious crisis since 1558. This stemmed mainly from the domestic issues of religion and succession, but the hostility of the catholic European powers made the situation particularly threatening.

Following her arrival in England, Mary Queen of Scots immediately became the catalyst of English court politics. In October 1568 a marriage between Mary and Thomas Howard, Duke of Norfolk, had been suggested to Norfolk by Maitland, one of the

Scottish Regent Moray's commissioners. Norfolk was sufficiently conservative in religion to appeal to Mary's catholicism, but he had conformed to the Anglican settlement so he secured the backing of prominent protestants on the council. Cecil was hostile and regarded Mary's prime aim as the 'recovery of the tyranny of Rome'. But other councillors, including protestants such as Throgmorton and Leicester, saw the marriage as the best solution to Mary's future and the succession problem. If Mary was restored to Scotland through English diplomacy and with an English husband, she would be forced to govern Scotland with moderation. Moreover, this would provide the basis of a lasting peace with Spain and France, and end England's dangerous isolation in Europe. Alongside the Norfolk marriage plans a conspiracy against Cecil was emerging. In the spring of 1569 Norfolk, Arundel and Leicester made a powerful attack on Cecil's aggressive policy towards Spain, with the aim (according to Fénélon, the French ambassador) of getting him imprisoned in the Tower (**49**). In addition, the northern militants, who were determined to force Elizabeth to make concessions to the catholics and to recognise Mary as her successor, were actively plotting throughout 1568–69.

By the summer of 1569 the prospect of the Norfolk marriage was fast receding. Negotiations with the Earl of Moray to restore Mary in Scotland, which were central to the marriage plans, had broken down by late July (**49**, p. 216). Elizabeth had shown her support for Cecil, and consequently the conspiracy to remove him was on the wane. It seems possible that a reconciliation took place between Norfolk and Cecil in mid 1569, after the Duke had received a favourable verdict over the Dacre inheritance in the Court of Wards (of which Cecil was the Master). Moreover, as time progressed, it became imperative to seek Elizabeth's approval for the marriage, and on 6 September Leicester told Elizabeth of their plans. She was furious and immediately summoned Norfolk to attend her at Windsor, but he ignored the summons and made for his estates in East Anglia. However, instead of raising his tenantry he spent a week of indecision and finally decided to throw himself on the Queen's mercy. On his way to London he sent a message to his brother-in-law, the Earl of Westmorland, instructing him not to rebel (**49**, pp. 211–20).

Ever since coming to England, Mary Queen of Scots had been in touch with the catholic Earl of Northumberland and his close supporters, Richard Norton and Leonard Dacre, but up to September 1569 there was no coherent plan for rebellion in the north. Northumberland, however, was in touch with the Spanish ambassador, de Spes, and in June 1569 it appears that the Earl promised to provide 15,000 men to restore Mary if Philip II would send a force to England. Ridolfi, a Florentine banker, maintained contact between the southern catholic nobility, the papacy, the Spanish ambassador and the Northern Earls. The Earl of Northumberland had been against the Norfolk marriage, hoping that Mary would marry Philip II instead. Only under instructions from Mary himself had he agreed to accept it.

The supporters of Mary Stuart in the north saw Norfolk's refusal to obey his summons to court as a signal for rebellion. When Norfolk submitted, neither of the leading Northern Earls, Northumberland and Westmorland, was keen to fight, but urged on by their followers and their wives, they rode to Durham, where on 14 November they pulled down the protestant communion table in the cathedral and ordered the celebration of the mass. If there had been widespread catholic resentment in the north, here was the opportunity to express it. There were some encouraging signs. For one thing, support was not confined to the followers of the Percies (Northumberland), the Nevilles (Westmorland) and the Dacres – indeed, only 10 per cent of those who joined the rebellion were tenants of these leading families. But in the upper levels of society there was little enthusiasm for the revolt. In Yorkshire only about eighty gentlemen joined, all from catholic families. The vast majority of the gentry were, as Sir Ralph Sadler reported on 30 November, 'very willinge and forwarde' in the Queen's service. The main rebellion was over before Christmas, though Lord Dacre raised 3,000 troops in January 1570 before he was defeated by Lord Hunsdon in a pitched battle between Carlisle and Hexham. A number of the rebel leaders escaped, including the Earl of Westmorland and his three sons. But the Earl of Northumberland was handed back to the English by the Scottish Regent in 1572 and executed at York (**36**, pp. 91–101).

The rebellion had arisen partly out of the tensions in northern society as well as individual grievances, but the religious issue was paramount and was stressed in all the proclamations issued by the Earls (**36**, pp. 101–6). The Earl of Northumberland was a passionate adherent of catholicism, and two of the main agitators in the revolt were Thomas Markenfeld and Dr Nicholas Morton, who had returned from the continent in 1568, inspired by the Counter Reformation. Moreover, if any issue could have given the rebellion wide appeal it was religion. As Ralph Sadler wrote of Yorkshire in

1569, 'the common people are ignorant, superstitious and altogether blinded with the old popish doctrine'. But Sadler also commented that 'though the hearts of the people were with the rebels their persons supported the government'. The outcome of the revolt might have been different if the Earls had possessed the necessary supplies and money to fight a winter campaign against a strong government force. And if they had taken a more determined military stance they might have encouraged wider resistance, and brought in people like Henry Clifford, Earl of Cumberland, who was a keen supporter of Mary Queen of Scots, but stood aloof. As it was, however, they failed to mobilise the religious conservatism of the north into an effective challenge to Elizabeth's government.

By the time the revolt broke out the papacy had decided to take a more positive attitude towards English affairs and was looking for a suitable opportunity to intervene. In March 1569 Pius V asked the Duke of Alva, the Spanish governor and army commander in the Netherlands, about the possibility of a joint invasion of England by Spanish and French forces. Alva, however, was fully occupied with his military campaign in the Netherlands and gave no encouragement. But in November of that year the Northern Earls wrote to Rome, asking for papal support. Encouraged by the news of their rebellion, and urged on by the catholic exiles in Louvain, the pope, on 22 February 1570, issued the Bull of Excommunication, *Regnans in Excelsis*, against Elizabeth.

The Bull of Excommunication deprived Elizabeth of 'her pretended title' of Supreme Head of the Church – a title which, in fact, she neither possessed nor claimed – and commanded her subjects not to obey her. It also warned English catholics that if they did not withdraw their obedience as instructed they would themselves incur the penalty of excommunication. In issuing this bull the papacy was exercising its right to depose heretical princes, a traditional claim of the papal 'fulness of power' (**79**). The most significant point about the bull was that no provision was made to ensure its enforcement by catholic powers, who were not even officially informed of its publication. Such a lack of basic diplomacy strongly suggests that the bull was not primarily meant as an invitation to the catholic princes to invade England. The papacy was relying on English catholics to put it into effect, even though no steps were taken to ensure the bull's official publication in England (**50**). It must be presumed that the papacy was ignorant of the collapse of the Northern Rebellion, but as it turned out the timing could hardly have been more inept.

15

The vast majority of English catholics decided to ignore the bull (**79**), which was to be expected. There were few supporters of papal supremacy among catholic families, and where catholicism drew heavily on conservative tradition in the remoter areas, papal interference was as unacceptable as that of the crown. Moreover the Northern Rebellion had shown that only a limited number of catholics were prepared to rebel. The effect of the bull was therefore fairly negative. There is some evidence, however, that it encouraged recusancy; in Lancashire, for example, there were reports of falling church attendances by October 1570. Through the efforts of Allen and Vaux, Lancashire had shown itself more sensitive than other areas to papal leadership and was perhaps the strongest of the catholic counties. Some individuals responded to the bull by becoming recusants. Edmund Plowden, a leading catholic lawyer, said that he worshipped in the Established Chuch until 1570 because the Common Prayer Book had not until then been condemned, which reflects the failure of papal communications up to this point. Some of the apparent increase in recusancy might also be explained in terms of greater detection, as there was a crackdown against catholics in 1570–71 in the dioceses of Norwich, Chester and Winchester.

The 1571′ Parliament passed a series of new statutes to protect Elizabeth from the effects of papal denunciation. The Treason Acts made it high treason to write or in any way to signify that Elizabeth was not the lawful Queen. Another act prohibited the bringing in or executing of any bull from Rome. This last statute had widespread implications, for anyone who reconciled an English subject to the see of Rome by means of a Papal Bull was also therefore guilty of treason. The mood of Parliament was unsympathetic towards catholicism. A bill advocated by Bishop Sandys for stiffer penalties against recusants, and more significantly for a 100 mark fine for not taking communion at least once a year, passed both Houses. Elizabeth, refusing to allow the Papal Bull to influence her established policy, vetoed the bill (**50**, p. 104). A year earlier, in June 1570, the Queen had assured English catholics that her intention was 'not to have any of them molested by any inquisition or examination of their consciences in the causes of religion' so long as they did not overtly break her laws (**50**, p. 104).

While the 1571 Parliament was in session, the web of another plot was being woven around Mary Queen of Scots. Certain ingredients were the same as in 1569. Ridolfi and Norfolk were again involved, while Spain and the papacy promised help. In 1571 Ridolfi received despatches from Rome promising financial backing from the papacy and military aid from Spain. By March the Norfolk marriage plan had been revived, with Norfolk, according to Ridolfi, giving verbal assurances that he was a Catholic. But the plot failed to materialise into an international enterprise, since Philip II showed his usual caution and withheld his help for a 'future occasion'. Among the English catholics there was a small uprising in Lancashire involving the younger sons of the Earl of Derby, but the loyalty of the Earl himself ensured its failure. By January 1572 the Duke of Norfolk was in the Tower on three charges of treason, and Ridolfi had quietly left the country (**50**).

The events of 1568–72 had an important effect on English politics. By 1572 the Council had lost two of the old aristocracy, the Earl of Arundel and the Duke of Norfolk, and its general composition was more protestant. The Northern Rebellion, the Papal Bull and the Ridolfi Plot doubtlessly heightened anti-catholic feeling, though to what degree is difficult to assess, as it seems unlikely that the mood of the House of Commons reflected opinion over the whole country. These years increased the likelihood of a catholic conspiracy on a European scale now that Mary Stuart could play a central role and that English friendship with Spain had been destroyed. Such conspiratorial fears seemed confirmed by the massacre of French protestants in Paris on the eve of the Feast of St Bartholomew in 1572. For all that, the impact of events on English catholics was probably slight. The majority had been moved neither by the Northern Earls nor the papacy to oppose their sovereign, while Elizabeth had vetoed the proposed harsher anti-catholic laws. Basically the position of the papists remained unchanged until they were exhorted to greater recusancy by the missionary priests of the late 1570s and the 1580s.

The most vigorous catholicism of these years was among the expatriates on the continent, particularly at Louvain. The literary output of the exiles was remarkable, though Nicholas Sander's claim that 20,000 copies of their works had been smuggled into England by 1580 is perhaps optimistic. Their efforts helped sustain the morale of English catholics, and in 1565 Jewel complained that 'the popish exiles are disturbing us and giving us all the trouble in their power'. Though many of the works were concerned with religious controversy, others were devotional. Thomas Harding translated a number of Spanish writings into English, familiarising English catholics with some of the spiritual works of the Counter Reformation. Some exiles were among the early advocates of using

17

force to restore English catholicism. But a more practical step was the founding of a seminary at Douai in the Netherlands by William Allen, who was an exile at Louvain before returning to his native Lancashire. Douai was established in 1568 to educate catholics abroad and later to train priests who would return to England. This was the first recognition of the prime role of the priesthood in sustaining catholicism in England. By 1573 the first priests had been ordained and some arrived in England the following year.

An assessment of the importance of Douai and the subsequent impact of the missionary priests is essential in interpreting the nature of English catholicism in the sixteenth century. Professor Bossy sees a new catholic community emerging after 1570, the novel creation of the missionary priests (**24**). This interpretation has been strongly challenged by Dr Haigh (**104**, **105**), who not only argues the case for the continuity of English catholicism in the sixteenth century [**doc. 7**], but also pinpoints the discontinuity argument to Robert Parsons, where it originated as a 'propagandist Jesuit version of Tudor Catholic history' (**105**). Since this debate is central to the issues discussed in this book, the theme will recur in chapters 2 and 4, but some points need to be made at this stage.

Unless a very narrow definition of catholicism is adopted, the evidence of catholic survival in the first decade or so of Elizabeth's reign is overwhelming. There was relatively little recusancy, partly because the separation of catholics from the parochial organisation only occurred gradually as parishes became fully protestantised, and partly because there was little encouragement for it from the clerical leadership. The small number of detected recusants is also a reflection of the inability of the authorities to persuade churchwardens to present recusants, especially in the most catholic areas; recusant numbers were doubtlessly higher than the records suggest. Not only was there a strong survival of conservative religious practices in certain areas, but there is a close link between such conservatism and later recusancy. This was true of Durham (**85**), while in Lancashire the later Elizabethan concentration of recusancy among the chapelries in the Blackburn deanery can be explained by the activities of half a dozen former Marian chaplains who by 1571 were saying masses for their erstwhile parishioners. Ripon in Yorkshire provides a good example of the conservative religion of the 1560s being translated into strong recusancy by the early seventeenth century. Dr Haigh (**105**) has effectively overturned Professor Dickens's conclusion on Yorkshire that 'between survivalism and seminarism little or no connection existed' (**82**,

p. 181). The fact that by 1577, before the seminary priests could have made an impact, there were some 1,500 recusants according to a government survey, shows that the process of separation had already begun. The task of the priests therefore was not to create a new catholicism but to develop that which had survived. That is not to deny the central role that the seminary priests were to play over the next half century.

Part Two: Descriptive Analysis

2 The Counter Reformation in England

The establishment of the mission

The founding of Douai was 'the first step towards turning the out-ward traffic of émigrés into an inward traffic of priests' (**73**, p. 136), and it was from Douai that the first 'missionary' priests arrived in England in 1574. But the continuity of English catholicism described in the last chapter raises doubts about the very concepts of 'mission' and 'missionaries', which designate a society recently converted to christianity, and also challenges the importance of the role of the seminary priests and the Jesuits. It has been argued that leaders of the mission such as Allen, Gerard and Parsons saw their task as that of reconciling 'schismatics' – i.e. making the existing body of catholic Church Papists into recusants rather than convert-ing heretics (**105**). But this task in itself was more decisive than anything attempted by the Marian priests, who seldom tried to in-sist on recusancy. Moreover, the stress on working through existing catholic strength was a matter of tactics rather than an ultimate objective. The commitment of Allen and Parsons to the reconver-sion of England was strong enough to lead them into supporting the idea of foreign invasion to accomplish it, as they gradually real-ised how enormous a task conversion by evangelising would be. It was only in the seventeenth century that the Jesuits' leadership accepted catholicism as a minority religion and on one level aban-doned the concept of a mission. Whether on another level they also saw the mission in terms of changing the spiritual direction of English catholicism will be discussed later (ch. 4).

The geographical location of Douai was significant for the future pattern of the English mission. It was in the extreme south-west of the Netherlands, in a French-speaking area, almost equidistant from Paris and Brussels. Though students occasionally travelled via Antwerp or Bruges, the natural route to England went through St Omer to Calais, Gravelines or Dunkirk. Moreover in 1578 the revolt of the Netherlands forced the seminary from Douai over the border into Rheims, so that between 1578 and 1590 the vast majority of priests came to England from French ports. Spain was only used on any scale after the outbreak of the final civil war in France in 1589. The seminary at Valladolid was established in 1589, and another seminary at Seville three years later reflected the growing importance of Spain for the English mission. Priests going from Spain to England often made use of intermediary ports such as Waterford and Cork in Ireland, or Nantes and La Rochelle in France (**73**).

The ports of departure on the continent naturally dictated the seminary priests' points of entry into England. Those using the Netherlands were likely to arrive in Hull, Newcastle or other ports along the east coast. Consequently reception places sprang up on that coast, such as Grosmont Priory near Whitby, well known as a shelter for priests by the early 1580s. Priests who used Calais or Dunkirk landed on the south coast and frequently made for London. The sea route from Spain was never as popular as the other two, even in the 1590s, but when it was used it landed priests in the south-west or at ports such as Chester (for those arriving via Ireland).

By 1575 some eleven secular priests had arrived from Douai and by 1580, before the arrival of the Jesuits, some 100 seculars had come to England. William Allen was most enthusiastic about the early successes of the priests, while Fr John Paine remarked that 'the heretics were as much troubled at the name of the Anglo-Douay priests which is now famous throughout England as all the catholics are consoled thereby'. The leadership provided by the seminary priests must have increased the morale of the English catholics even if optimistic comments, such as Allen's assertion in 1577 that 'the numbers of those who were daily restored to the catholic church almost surpassed belief', have to be taken sceptically (**3**).

In the development of the English mission the Jesuits, despite their small number, made a vital contribution. Though the first missionary priests had arrived in England in 1574, the mission itself had little or no organisation in its first decade. When Willian Anlaby of Elton in Yorkshire entered his native country in 1578 he worked alone, carrying his mass kit on his back and travelling on foot. Later he acquired a horse and joined forces with William Atkinson, a fellow Yorkshireman. When the Jesuit Robert Parsons arrived in London in 1580 there was no organisation to receive him and he was 'forced with great danger of being discovered to go up and down half a day until noon, at what time he resolved to adventure into the prison of Marshalsea and to ask for a gentleman prisoner Thomas Pound, in whose chambers he dined and was singularly comforted with the sight not only of him, but of many of his confessors . . .' (**3**). Thomas Pound introduced Parsons to a group of catholic gentlemen, led by George Gilbert, who were prepared to assist the mission. By the time Campion arrived in London some ten days after Parsons, 24 June 1580, Gilbert and his friends had already made plans to meet him. Nevertheless the hazards of the early mission were great [**doc. 4**].

Parsons tried to correct the lack of organisation over the next few years. London was developed as an important base and centre of distribution for incoming priests, while in the counties there was an attempt to develop known shelters for priests on a more systematic basis. As early as July 1580 Campion and Parsons attended a synod at Southwark, where the two most important questions discussed were the attendance of catholics at Anglican services and the problem of organising the mission. Attendance at Anglican services was condemned as a grave sin, and although no concrete suggestions emerged on missionary organisation, the problem was recognised.

When Parsons left England in 1581 he was convinced that improved organisation was the most pressing need of the English mission. By 1584 he had established a scheme for sending priests from Europe to England. Rouen was the centre of Parsons's operations, since it was 'a most convenient town on account of its nearness to the sea, so that there some can make trips to the coast to arrange for boats to convey people across'. Moreover, Rouen was close to the seminary at Rheims. Allen sent the priests, and Parsons arranged their crossing. The organising of the missionaries once they reached England was also under way, as Parsons explained in a letter to the Jesuit General in 1584 concerning the sending of two Jesuits into England. 'As to the way of staying or living in England I cannot prescribe any other than that which has been followed up to now, and which other priests keep. One of them will have to live mostly in London or near it in order to direct others' (**22**, p. 71).

Parsons made the most careful preparations for the entry into England of the Jesuit William Weston and a lay brother Ralph Emerson. 'I arranged for a special boat to be at their disposal,' he wrote, 'and managed also that an English gentleman who was staying here and has properties on the English coast should enter the country with them for the sole purpose of guiding them safely to his house; afterwards he and his servant will come back.' The missionaries were to be accompanied as far as London 'where there are many houses now fitted to receive them' (**22**, p. 71). In March 1585 Parsons moved to St Omer, possibly because Rouen was becoming well known to Walsingham's spies. Allen continued to send priests from Rheims, but in July 1585 Parsons went to Rome. After this date, evidence on the organisation which despatched priests from the continent is fragmentary. Isolated evidence suggests that the methods pioneered at Rouen and St Omer – the avoidance of public boats and the making for London after an initial stay in the south or south-east – were continued. Precise routes depended, of course, on the European political situation.

By 1585 there is evidence of greater organisation on the English mission. At a conference in Hoxton on the outskirts of London a number of seminary priests met prominent catholic gentry. Henry Vaux, son of Lord Edward Vaux, a staunch Northamptonshire catholic aristocrat, was appointed to look after missionary finances, and it was agreed that priests should try to avoid too much reliance on the catholic gentry in times of great persecution. But priests were still being lost at an alarming rate. Between 1581 and 1586 thirty priests had been executed and fifty were in prison – more than half the priests who had entered the country. Moreover, though certain areas, in particular London, had been established to receive incoming priests, the distribution of seminarists across the country was still defective. In July 1586 William Weston complained that 'there are three or four counties together as yet unfurnished with priests . . . the tops have been left and only the lower boughs dealt with'. Another Jesuit, Robert Southwell, made the same point: 'it is to be regretted that in many counties, containing no small number of catholics, there is not a single priest' (**25**, p. 35).

It was mainly due to the work of Robert Southwell and his fellow Jesuit Henry Garnet that the English mission was put on a more secure basis in the years following their arrival in 1586. Southwell's task was to stay in London to assist new arrivals while Garnet toured the country strengthening catholic contacts. Garnet kept in touch with Southwell by coming to London twice a year, usually in spring and summer (**25**, p. 65), and by 1596 he was expressing satisfaction at the development of the priestly network. 'When the priests first arrive from the seminaries we give them every help we can. The greater part of them, as opportunity offers, we place in fixed residences. This is done in a very large number of families through our offices. The result now is that many persons who saw a seminary priest hardly once a year, now have one all the time and most eagerly welcome any others, no matter where they come from' (**25**, p. 45).

After Southwell's capture in 1592 and his subsequent execution, the full burden of organisation fell on Garnet. Between then and 1605 Garnet rented a number of houses in London which provided shelter for incoming priests. The most celebrated of these, White Webbs at Enfield in Middlesex, was an important centre of catholic life, as a French visitor remarked when he 'found Garnet in the company with several Jesuits and gentlemen, who were playing music, among them Mr William Byrd, who played the organ and many other instruments. To that house came, chiefly on solemn days observed by the papists, many of the nobility and many ladies by coach or otherwise' (**25**, p. 317).

Despite the improvements, however, regional organisation was still a problem in the 1590s. John Gerard was put in charge of East Anglia until his arrest and subsequent escape from the Tower, after which the secular priest John Bavand seems to have replaced him. Garnet tried to supervise the East Midlands himself, but after 1592 he was increasingly in London. In the West Midlands, Edward Oldcorn made Hinlip Hall in Worcestershire the centre of local organisation from 1589 until his arrest there in January 1606. The Yorkshire mission began in 1582, with Thomas Bell acting as *de facto* leader before John Mush, later one of the Appellants, took over. Mush established a route from Middelburg in Flanders to South Shields during the 1580s. A reception house at South Shields was run by one Ursula Taylor, while Lawrence Vellan, who had spent some time at Douai, met priests and supplied them with money. The Jesuit Richard Holtby put the mission on a more secure basis after 1591. He developed the existing Middelburg to South Shields run. Newly arrived priests were passed from South Shields to Holtby's refuge at Thornley, Durham, and thence south to Grosmont Priory (**19**, pp. 158–9).

The role of the catholic gentry in the establishment and development of the English mission was vital, and complemented that of the priests. From 1580, when Edmund Campion was received by a group of young laymen, to the involvement of the younger Vaux in missionary finances in 1585, the laity were involved at all stages of organisation. The ability of English gentry to offer the necessary protection to the outlawed priests has long been recognised as a crucial element in the revival of catholicism. No less important, the gentry had the necessary social contacts both within and outside their own counties, which enabled them to organise catholic circuits with the help of the priests. Occasionally contemporary accounts show such a circuit at work. Thomas Barcroft, a seminary priest, arrived in England in October 1589. He stayed a month in London, first at the White Horse Inn in Fleet Street and then in Enfield with John Townley, a prominent Lancashire recusant. Through Townley's efforts the priest was sent to Lady Hesketh in Martholme, in Lancashire, where he built up his acquaintance among Lancashire catholics. He subsequently stayed with a Mr Yates, a Blackburn schoolmaster, and with Henry Hindley of Pendle Forest, where he baptised a Hindley child. By 1591 Barcroft was back in London, probably trying to make arrangements to work in another county. His experience cannot have been untypical (**1**).

Itinerant missionary priests were still to be found in the seventeenth century, but the English mission already had the basis of a national organisation by the end of the Elizabethan period. The appointment of the Archpriest Blackwell in 1598 had relatively little impact on this organisation, but it does symbolise the more settled nature of the mission. The significance of the Elizabethan seminarists and Jesuits is now the subject of sharply differing opinions. John Bossy sees the construction of the mission as a major achievement, stressing in particular the work of Garnet. 'Garnet, in his long period of office in conditions that were unpromising from a number of viewpoints, constructed a working organisational machinery which provided a model for his successors, whether they appreciated this or not' (**24**, p. 204). Christopher Haigh, on the other hand, argues that later Elizabethan and Stuart catholicism should not be viewed as 'the successful product of missionary triumph in the face of protestantism and persecution. It was a rump community, the residue of a process of failure and decline in which whole regions and social groups were neglected...' (**106**, p. 132).

Dr Haigh has provided a number of new insights in this challenging article, but his judgement seems too harsh. The limited nature of the missionary achievement is clear; the priests were unsuccessful not only in their ultimate aim of reconverting England, but even in the more specific task of fully transforming existing conservative religion into a separated, recusant catholicism. There was a decline of catholicism in areas such as the north-west in the late Elizabethan period (see ch. 4) and popular catholicism probably declined as gentry domination increased. The missionary structure was biased in favour of the south-east, whereas catholic strengths were in the north. In 1580 half of the seminary priests working in

England were in Essex, London and the Thames Valley areas which together probably had not more than a fifth of detected recusants, while the north had two-fifths (**105**).

However, certain points need to be stressed. The conditions which had sustained the catholic survival in the 1560s and 1570s – namely the Marian recusant priests and a high number of conservative Elizabethan clergy, which made possible a 'catholicism within the Elizabethan church' – were changing. Without the efforts of the seminary priests, catholicism would eventually have all but disappeared. The geographical bias towards the south-east was partly determined by the location of the main seminaries on the continent, but also by a realisation that if a national organisation was to be established, the obvious centre was London. The size of London, its cosmopolitan population and good communications, made it a successful base for the Jesuit and later the secular priests' organisation. The domination by the gentry, a class who could provide shelter and finance for the priests, was almost inevitable, as the parishes even in the remoter areas became gradually protestantised. Indeed Dr Haigh concedes that 'perhaps it was always likely that the attempt to practise Counter Reformation piety in conditions of proscription would lead the missionaries into the arms of the gentry, and that the catholic minority would become a seigneurially-structured minority' (**106**, p. 147).

The expansion of recusancy

The position of catholicism was changing in the 1580s under the impact of the work of the missionary priests on the one hand and more intense persecution on the other. Although it is impossible to quantify these changes in the 1580s and 1590s, it seems probable that there was a decrease in the number of families which, because of their conservative beliefs and reluctance to accept the innovations of the Elizabethan Church, could be called catholics. Yet it is equally clear that there was a marked increase in the number of committed catholics, especially recusants. Changes in Sussex illustrate the trend. In the 1560s there were probably some thirty-three catholic families among the leading gentry. By the 1580s the number had been reduced to twenty-five, but of these fifteen were recusant. This trend continued into the 1590s, which saw a further reduction in the number of catholic gentry but a slight increase in recusancy (**52**, p. 259).

Sussex, however, was not entirely typical of catholic fortunes, since it was a county where protestant influence was growing. The significant expansion of recusancy can be demonstrated from those counties where the old faith was strongest. In Lancashire the increase in recusancy was dramatic. The Archiepiscopal Visitation of 1578 recorded 304 recusants, yet by 1590 this had risen to 534, a figure which probably underestimates real recusant strength. By the first year of James's reign the number had risen to over 3,500. Dr Haigh, in his book on religious developments in Tudor Lancashire, summarises these trends. 'Though one may doubt whether the contrast between the 1560s and 1570s on the one hand and the 1580s and 1590s on the other hand were as marked as some have suggested, it is nevertheless true that there was a considerable expansion of recusancy after 1578' (**40**, p. 269).

Exactly the same pattern can be seen in the East Riding of Yorkshire. There were some 40 adult recusants and 70 non-communicants in the period 1570–78, but these had increased to about 200 adult recusants and possibly some 150 Church Papists by the 1590s. Though these figures are small compared with the total population in the Riding, which could muster 10,000 able-bodied men in 1584, the preponderance of gentry made catholicism a strong force there. Moreover, recusancy increased over the whole of Yorkshire in the late Elizabethan period and by 1604 there were 112 recusant gentry families, probably double the number of the early 1580s. This increased recusancy did not necessarily mean a major shift of religious beliefs within the county, as one recent historian of Yorkshire has pointed out. 'If the number of recusant families was growing, this does not mean that there had been any significant gains from protestantism. What we are witnessing is a polarisation process within the catholic gentry; one section was going over completely to Anglicanism while another section was becoming fully and irrevocably committed to the old Religion' (**28**, p. 189).

In most areas the achievement of the missionary priests in producing the expansion of recusancy was based on existing catholic inclinations, building on the work of the Marian priests and upon individual and communal commitment to the old faith. But there were also places where catholicism was actually created by the seminary priests, especially in urban centres such as London. There the prisons, Inns of Court, embassy chapels and visiting catholic gentry provided pockets of catholicism in the 1570s. But it was only later, especially in the 1590s, that an indigenous population of recusants – gentry, professional classes and artisans –

emerged. Except for the years of severe persecution from 1588 to 1592, recusancy in London and Middlesex rose steadily in the late Elizabethan period. In 1587 some 60 recusants had been convicted, but by 1603 the figure was over 700. It is true that these numbers were swollen by catholic gentry from the counties who were imprisoned in London, but the emergence of a non-gentry body of recusants was a tribute to the work of the seminary priests.

The increased rate of detection must be taken into account in the expansion of recusancy in the 1580s and 1590s as the persecution of catholics increased. But this is not the full or even the main explanation. The first objective of the missionary priests was the reconciliation of 'schismatics'; Church Papists were to be persuaded into recusancy. In particular, when priests were appointed as domestic chaplains, the entire household was likely to become recusant, except possibly for its head, who might still attend Anglican services occasionally to avoid recusancy fines. It was Lord Montague's chaplain, Robert Gray, who convinced him of the necessity of recusancy in the 1580s (see p. 7). A similar development can be seen within the Bellamy family who lived in Uxendon, Harrow-on-the-Hill, near London. In the 1560s and 1570s they practised catholicism within the parish; the registers show that all members of the family were baptised, married and buried in the parish church. But in the 1580s Uxendon became a centre for missionary priests, starting with Campion in 1581 and ending with the capture of Southwell in 1592. Mrs Bellamy and her son Jerome were convicted for recusancy for the first time in 1583. In 1586 both were imprisoned for giving shelter to Anthony Babington (see p. 34), while two other sons were imprisoned in the 1580s, one for 'refusing to take the Queen's part against the pope's army and refusing to take the Oath [of Supremacy]'. By the 1590s the family had been entirely ruined by its commitment to catholicism – a commitment which before 1580 had not amounted to recusancy.

Government policy 1580–1603

'The obstinate and stiff-necked papist is so far from being reformed as he hath gotten stomach to go backwards and show his disobedience not only in arrogant words but also in contemptuous deeds...' (**1**). Such was the opinion of Sir Walter Mildmay in 1581. Fears about popery were particularly understandable in the early 1580s since the efforts of the missionary priests to revitalise catholicism were taking place against a deteriorating international situation. In

1579–80 there was a danger of papal and Spanish intervention in Ireland, while the revival of French influence in Scotland raised the possibility of a catholic European enterprise against England. The extreme catholic faction in France led by the Guises planned an invasion of England, in which Parsons, Allen and a number of catholic exiles were involved. Against such a background it is hardly surprising that the English government took severe measures to limit catholicism. The extent to which the 12d. fine for church absence was ever effectively enforced is still an open question, but it was an insufficient deterrent in the face of the new missionary effort of the seminary priests. A new penalty was needed to back up the Act of Uniformity.

The harshness of the first bill produced by Parliament in 1581 to check the increased recusancy reflected the deep concern of both Houses. This bill made the saying of mass a felony punishable by death, while refusing to come to church for the fourth time would incur the punishment of *praemunire*. Another bill introduced in the Lords with the support of the bishops would have made the taking of communion rather than attendance at church the test of comformity. Neither bill became law, the former probably due to the Queen's intervention, the latter possibly because of the Commons' suspicion of ecclesiastical power. The statute which emerged, 'An Act to retain the Queen's Majesty's subjects in their due obedience', was harsh, though less so than the bills discussed. The statute laid down that any 'person who acted to withdraw any of the Queen's Majesty subjects... from their natural obedience to her Majesty, or to withdraw them for that intent from the religion now by her Highness' authority established... to the Romish religion, or move them to promise any pretended authority of the see of Rome, shall be to all intents adjudged to be traitors' (**50**, pp. 175–6).

Historians have differed over the interpretation of this statute. Meyer and Neale (**55, 57**) both argue that the Act made it treason to convert or to be converted to Rome only if this was done with the intention of withdrawing the subject from his or her obedience to the Queen. McGrath, however, concludes that 'the law does seem to treat as treason *in itself* the act of reconciling or being reconciled to the Pope's authority' (**50**). The Act is certainly ambiguous, which was possibly deliberate. It linked the religious activities of the seminary priests and their potential converts with the committing of treason. There was no attempt to apply this to every catholic reconciled to Rome, but it remained as a threat, and provided a legal basis previously lacking for the Elizabethan government's attack on the seminary priests.

Of the other provisions in the 1581 statute, the most important was the £20 per month fine for 'every person above the age of sixteen years which shall not repair to some church, chapel or usual place of common prayer'. The year 1581 marks the start of a harsher policy towards catholics. In that year four priests were executed, while in 1582 eleven more executions followed. But despite the severity of this new legislation, it would be wrong to deny any continuity between Elizabethan policy in the 1580s and that of earlier years. Elizabeth aimed to eliminate the seminary priests by the most inquisitorial methods, but her intention towards the laity was still to push them – albeit somewhat harder – into Anglican conformity.

However much Elizabeth wished to continue the policy of her early years, events at home and abroad demanded harsher measures. The number of missionary priests increased; 179 arrived in England between 1580 and 1585. In 1584 William of Orange was assassinated. This not only raised fears for Elizabeth's safety, but increased the likelihood of a Spanish victory in the Netherlands. By December 1584 the Catholic League in France had allied itself to Philip II, and the Catholic Enterprise against protestant England seemed imminent.

Consequently it is hardly surprising that when Parliament met at the end of 1585 one member felt that the Pope was 'knitting together all the papish princes and states to the overthrow of the Gospel in all places, but especially in this kingdom'. Parliament's response to this threat was 'An Act against Jesuits, seminary priests and such other like disobedient persons'. This statute of 1585 declared that any priest who had been ordained by the Pope's authority was guilty of treason once he came to England. Any person who should 'willingly and wittingly receive, relieve, comfort or maintain' any such priest or religious person was guilty of felony and might be sentenced to death (**50**, p. 192). This was the harshest piece of legislation of the period. Out of 146 catholics executed between 1586 and 1603, no less than 123 were indicted under this statute.

Further legislation was enacted in 1587, by which time the inadequacies and ineffectiveness of the 1581 statute had become apparent. Few recusants had paid the £260 per year fine (calculated on the basis of thirteen months to a year). The Exannual Rolls of the Exchequer show the extent of bad debt already accumulated under the 1581 statute. Moreover, other recusants 'escape indicting through the corruptness of juries', as one member of Parliament protested. Therefore a new Act was passed to make the 1581 statute more effective. Though it embodied no new principles, important changes were made. Fines levied on recusants were not limited to a specific conviction, but were cumulative from the date of the first conviction. Also the fines were backdated to 1581 so that recusants such as Thomas Tresham and John Townley found themselves indebted for some £1,000 each by 1587. To ease the pressure on the courts, recusants could be convicted by proclamation in their absence if they failed to appear to answer the indictment. To ensure that fines were levied more efficiently, local assize courts which convicted the recusants had to send lists of them to the Exchequer by the end of the same law term; previously no time limit had been laid down. But the greatest practical change was the provision that two-thirds of the recusants' lands could be seized by the Exchequer if the recusants failed to pay their fines. More catholics suffered under this provision than under almost any other penal legislation (**101**).

The 1580s saw a build-up of persecution, especially after the Parliament of 1584–85 [**doc. 5**], which reached a climax in the years of the Armada and threatened invasions, 1588–92. In 1593 an 'Act against Popish Recusants' limited recusants' mobility to within five miles of their dwelling place, a measure designed to prevent the common practice of moving about to avoid imprisonment and fining. Parliament altered the original bill considerably. This had advocated extreme measures such as the taking away of children from recusant parents at the age of seven so that they could be educated in the protestant faith. Moreover, recusants would have been excluded from all the professions. If the original bill had been passed, catholics could well have been 'rendered impotent by virtual expropriation and exclusion from all influential vocations and eradicated in a single generation' (**57**).

How effective was the action taken by the Elizabethan government against the catholics? Lord Chief Justice Popham, writing in 1599, was convinced that even tougher measures were necessary. 'I see no waye to reduce these [recusants] to better conformytie and obedyence unless it may seeme good to the Lords [of the Council] eyther to have them detayned in close prison ... or to have the othe ministered to some of them first and so second tyme.' Refusal to accept the Oath of Supremacy twice meant the death penalty. Many modern historians have endorsed Popham's judgement.

F. X. Walker, in his unpublished thesis 'The Implementation of the Elizabethan Statutes against Recusants', concludes that the 1581 and 1587 statutes were failures, for despite the more efficient enforcement of anti-recusant measures 'there was no sign that a large section of recusants had been induced to change their convictions from fear of financial loss. No single document, no report of the Council ... so much as hints at such a development' (**101**).

Walker's conclusion is confirmed by the increased recusancy of the late Elizabethan period. There were plenty of good reasons for this, especially in the often lax administration of anti-recusant policies at local level. Of 800 recusants presented at the Lancaster assizes in 1592, only 200 were eventually indicted, and of these only 11 paid recusancy fines. Some remained in Lancaster gaol, but Bishop Vaughan complained that 'prisoners were allowed to go hunting, hawking and racing and they even carried arms in the streets of the town' (**40**, p. 289). A report on Chester in 1590 complained that of many hundred recusants indicted in recent years, few stood trial, because of their kinship with, and generous treatment by, the justices. As a result, the county was 'mightily infected with popery' (**97**).

It would be wrong, however, to dismiss Elizabethan policy as entirely ineffective. The very complexity of the policy makes judgement difficult. At one level the policy was vigorous – especially in attacking priests and their helpers. In 1588 alone, 21 priests and 16 lay people were put to death, and between 1590 and 1603 88 catholics were executed, 53 of them priests. Under the more tolerant policy of the Stuarts, English catholicism expanded because of the great increase in the number of priests.

Before 1581 the task of detecting and punishing catholics was largely in the hands of the ecclesiastical authorities. After this date, however, the main instrument used by the Elizabethan government to reduce the catholic gentry to conformity was the enforcement of the financial penalties prescribed by the statutes of 1581 and 1587. Initial examination of the effects of this campaign suggests that it was a failure. No more than sixteen recusants paid the full £260 per year levied by the 1581 statute. It has been estimated that in many counties no more than a tenth of convicted recusants suffered loss of land or goods when they failed to pay the £20 per month fine. But a number of qualifications must be made. The government always envisaged a large section of poorer recusants who could not pay a monthly fine, and there is evidence that in some areas at least the 12d. fine continued to be used for the punishment of such people. Moreover, historians have generally underestimated the extent to which the 1587 statute produced conformity among heads of households within the recusant body. The evidence of the Consistory Courts and of the Lord Treasurer's Remembrance Rolls catalogues such conformity. Even after the great expansion of recusancy in the 1580s and 1590s, occasional conformity by heads of households was essential for financial survival, and it is wrong to differentiate too strongly between Church Papists and recusants. J. T. Cliffe has argued that in Yorkshire most recusant gentry families had a 'schismatic' element. Such schismatic gentry could be catholic in all other respects, maintaining chaplains and sending their children abroad to be educated in catholic schools. Two of the recusants paying the full £260 per year in Elizabeth's reign, Sir Henry James of Kent and Jane Shelley of London, conformed early in the next reign. Sir Henry's conformity was short-lived, and he spent his last ten years in prison for refusing James I's Oath of Allegiance. Jane Shelley conformed after 1606, when under new legislation the government decided to seize two-thirds of her considerable estates rather than take the £260. Despite her conformity, she continued in her catholicism, leaving a handsome contribution to the English Mission on her death.

It is true that in practice the financial penalties were less heavy than they might have been. It was an almost universal practice for a recusant's land to be undervalued by local juries, so that the nominal two-thirds seized by the Exchequer was nowhere near two-thirds of its real worth. In certain northern counties, though not necessarily everywhere, the lease of two-thirds of the recusant's property was often acquired by a relative or a friend. In such cases, financial loss was minimal. But when all this has been said, the Exchequer of Receipt shows an increased revenue from recusants in the 1590s, and records reveal their subsequent conformity. Half the recusants whose lands or goods were earmarked by the Exchequer for seizure in London and Middlesex in the 1590s conformed before they suffered any financial loss.

The effect of the 1587 statute was to create more schismatics among heads of households than would have otherwise existed. Some schismatics, such as the Leeke family of Edmonton, Middlesex, had become Anglicans by 1640, but most remained committed catholics. The fiscal measures failed to eliminate catholicism and it is difficult to gauge the extent to which they checked its growth, though they certainly provided some restraint. Moreover if Elizabeth failed to eliminate catholicism, the majority of the catholic laity refused to question the Queen's authority and follow the line laid down by Parsons and Allen. Indeed by 1592 it seems that Allen had accepted that there would be a schismatic element among English catholics, despite his emphasis on the need for recusancy [**doc. 8**] and even though the Church Papists remained a butt for contemporary comment [**doc. 9**].

Catholics in English society: plots and tensions

The growing political tension in Europe in the early 1580s again brought Mary Queen of Scots to the centre of domestic and European politics. After the scare over Ireland in 1579–80, danger now threatened from Scotland between 1581 and 1583 when Esmé Stuart, a relative of the Duke of Guise, found favour with James VI. Various 'enterprises' against England involving Scotland and the Guises were planned. Allen, Parsons and William Holt, another Jesuit, were all deeply involved, and Holt hailed such an enterprise as a preparation for a religious war against England and the liberation of Mary Queen of Scots. Among the conspirators was an English catholic, Francis Throgmorton, who was arrested by Walsingham in November 1583. Throgmorton revealed that the proposed invasion, by French catholic forces, was to come through Sussex, and that Spain and the papacy had agreed to finance the scheme. All that remained to set off the enterprise was to rouse the English catholics. Parsons was all in favour of pressing ahead with this project, with Spanish help, but after Throgmorton's trial in May 1584 and the arrest of William Crichton, another Jesuit, the enterprise was abandoned.

In the wake of the assassination of William of Orange in the Netherlands, the Elizabethan government took all rumours of plots very seriously. In 1585 a Dr Parry was accused of organising a conspiracy, backed by the papacy, to assassinate the Queen. It is possible that Parry was an *agent provocateur*, but he was found guilty of treason and executed. In 1586 Anthony Babington, a young catholic gentleman, enlisted a number of fellow catholics in a scheme to free Mary and assassinate Elizabeth. The distinctive feature of the Babington Plot was that it was hatched on English soil, and only one ex-priest, John Ballard, was involved. Walsingham knew of the plot in its early stages; in fact room was made available in advance for the plotters in some London prisons. Babington was executed, along with twelve others. None of the plots of the 1580s represented a serious threat to the government and none had any widespread support among catholics, but all conspiracies compromised the reputation of the English catholics (**50**, p. 190 ff; **45**, p. 200 ff).

The issue of catholic loyalty to the state had already been raised in print. William Cecil's *The Execution of Justice in England*, published in 1583, tried to justify the execution of nineteen priests and laymen over the previous two years. The pamphlet argued that missionary priests were not punished for their religion; they were punished for their political actions in absolving English subjects from their obedience to the Queen, a point enshrined in the 1581 statute. Cecil argued that the refusal of priests to answer directly such questions as whether they thought all catholics should obey the Bull of Excommunication, whether they should consider Elizabeth their lawful Queen, and what part they should take if the Pope invaded England, rendered them treasonable. But, said Cecil, they were not in fact condemned on this point. They were condemned because 'they came . . . to contact those who would be ready to rebel and to poison the senses of the subjects, pouring into their hearts malicious and pestilent opinions against the Queen . . .' (**50**, p. 178).

For the majority of seminary priests, Cecil's assertions were totally unjust. The priests were not purveyors of international conspiracy. In 1584 William Allen replied for the catholics with his *'True Sincere and Modest Defense of English Catholics . . . wherein is declared how unjustly the protestants do charge the English Catholics with treason'*. Allen argued that English catholics were loyal and that they had not sought the excommunication of their Queen. The Pope, said Allen, did have the right to depose princes, but this need not be of great concern to English catholics (**50**, p. 184). This assertion was somewhat unconvincing in the light of the papal excommunication of 1570. Moreover, the deep involvement of Allen in plots to overthrow the Elizabethan government made his *Defense*, for all its skilful arguments, seem hollow. It is true that Allen tried to keep separate his two main concerns, the training of seminary priests and his political activities against England, but he intended to bring them together in the long run (**91**).

The catholic laity made their own collective declaration of allegiance to Elizabeth in an unsuccessful attempt to stop the Queen giving royal assent to the 1581 statute. It was composed by Sir Thomas Tresham, a leading recusant, and presented to the Queen in the name of two eminent catholics, Lord Henry Vaux and Sir John Arundell. This declaration asserted the loyalty of English catholics to Elizabeth and her lawful successors. However, the situation was not as straightforward as this declaration implied. All catholics needed priests to administer the sacraments, which were the main instruments of salvation. But these same priests refused to allow catholics to attend Anglican services, though the idea that priests might be urging the catholic gentry to renounce their allegiance to Elizabeth was held to be unthinkable. (**24**, p. 38).

In the Armada year of 1588 the catholic laity showed its loyalty, and many leading recusants expressed their desire to fight the Spaniards. This stance was taken despite the enthusiastic support given to the Armada by William Allen. In his *Declaration of the sentence and deposition of Elizabeth the usurper and pretensed Queen of England* (1588), Allen urged the English catholics to 'unite themselves to the catholic army' of Spain. But a secular priest named Wright justified the position taken by the catholic laity. English catholics could rightfully take up arms against Spain, he said, since Spain was invading for political, not religious, reasons. Though Wright did not reject the papal deposing power, he considered papal support for the Armada to be misplaced (**50**, p. 277, **60**, pp. 62–4).

In an effort to achieve toleration from James I, the catholic gentry made a further declaration of loyalty in their *Petition Apologetical* printed in 1604. The petition, again probably the work of Tresham, proposed that the number of catholic priests in the country should be reduced, and that every gentleman who kept a priest in his house should assume absolute civil responsibility for his behaviour. Moreover, priests should take an oath of allegiance 'before they shall be admitted to our houses, otherwise they shall not have relief of us' (**24**, p. 38; **64**, iv, p. 82).

The loyalty of English catholics to the state gave rise to certain tensions between the laity and some of the priests, especially the Jesuits. It was one of the issues, though not the central one, in the conflict among priests known as the Archpriest Controversy. Divisions among the priests first came to light at Wisbech prison. In 1588 the prisoners appear to have split into two groups, one under the spiritual authority of the Jesuit William Weston, and the other led by the secular priests Bagshaw and Bluet. The issues are far from clear. The secular priests seem to have resented Weston's natural leadership and the superior pose of his supporters. Bagshaw objected to the proposal that people should sit at meals as they arrive, regardless of status, 'a thing not practised in any ordered place in the world: a disgrace of all degree and learning and fit for Anabaptists'. The proposal offended the seculars' sense of strict hierarchy (**24**, pp. 35–49).

It was against this background of conflict and suspicion that the problem of providing an effective ecclesiastical leadership for the English mission was discussed. This had become particularly pressing after William Allen's death in 1594. Parsons, who enjoyed a good deal of influence at Rome, proposed the appointment of two bishops, assisted by archpriests, one resident in the Netherlands, the other in England. This scheme was rejected, however, as was a proposal by some of the secular clergy to form an association to elect one of themselves as bishop. Parsons then put forward an alternative plan; that an archpriest be appointed with limited jurisdiction over the secular clergy in Scotland and England. This suggestion was accepted, and on 7 March 1598 George Blackwell was appointed archpriest.

The office of archpriest was novel, and it offended the sense of dignity and conservatism of the leading secular priests. 'It is a mockery that you call it an ancient dignity in Christ's Church who knoweth not? The question is not of the ancientness of the dignity but of this new and never before heard of jurisdiction and authority.' Moreover, since the office was Parsons' idea, some seculars believed that Blackwell was a Jesuit appointment. A further cause of bitterness resulted from the wording of the Brief of Appointment, which recommended Blackwell to work closely with the Jesuits and tactlessly praised the Jesuit missionary work while omitting any reference to the numerically far greater efforts of the secular priests (**8**).

If the circumstances of Blackwell's appointment were unpromising, his initial actions were provocative, ensuring the outright hostility of leading secular priests, two of whom – William Bishop and Robert Charnock – appealed to Rome against Blackwell in 1598. The dispute dragged on, and the 'Appellants' made repeated representations to the Pope, including one by Bluet in 1601. The Pope issued his final decision on the whole question in 1602, a decision which made considerable concessions to the Appellants. Blackwell was ordered not to exceed his authority, not to consult with the Jesuits, but to report directly to Rome, and to take three Appellants as assistants.

Meanwhile one of the Appellants, William Watson, had begun to negotiate with the English government, hoping to achieve some form of toleration. In April 1599 Watson presented to the Attorney General a denunciation of the Jesuits for attempting to secure a Spanish succession to the throne. In a pamphlet of 1601, Watson argued that Elizabeth had treated catholics mildly, and that they therefore ought to be more loyal to 'our true and lawfull Queene and towards our countrie than hath bene taken and pursued by many catholickes, especially by the Jesuits'. In 1602 Watson proposed that the Appellants should take an oath of allegiance to the state, but many of the Appellants considered such an oath dangerous, arguing that it could compromise their role as priests. They therefore rejected the oath, but thirteen priests did agree to a Protestation of Allegiance in 1603, in which they gave a limited assurance of loyalty 'as any catholic priest can or ought to give unto their sovereign'. This Protestation was made despite a proclamation of 5 November 1602 which made it clear that the government would not tolerate two religions within the state. The hope that Henry IV of France, who supported the Appellants because of their anti-Spanish policies, could persuade Elizabeth to follow the French example of the Edict of Nantes, had been dashed (**75**).

The Appellant Protestation of 1603 was seen by A. O. Meyer as a victory for the Elizabethan government and the modern state, since the Appellants rejected the Allen-Parsons tradition of hostility to the state. While this is true, there is an initial irony in seeing the Appellants – those who appealed to Rome – as English nationalists. Moreover, the Archpriest Controversy was essentially an argument over ecclesiastical government, in which the issue of loyalty to the state was secondary. Only thirty-three Appellants signed the protest against the Jesuits at Wisbech in November 1600, and only thirteen out of some four hundred priests put their names to the 1603 Protestation. The Appellants remained a small party; the catholic gentry was unaffected in the earlier stages of the controversy, and many of the secular priests remained close to the Jesuits because the latter controlled so much of the English missionary organisation. However, an identity of interests did emerge between the Appellants and some of the leading catholic gentry after the death of Elizabeth. Tresham and others, hoping for toleration from James, were anxious to demonstrate their allegiance, and if this entailed getting rid of the Jesuits, it was a price they were willing to pay. The Appellants' main aim was also to attack the Jesuits, and a declaration of allegianace was a means to achieve this.

The Appellants and the Jesuits disagreed on matters of ecclesiastical government. Though there were different strands among the Appellants, they shared certain assumptions. They believed in a continuity between the pre-Reformation church in England and Elizabethan catholicism. They considered themselves to be the same body of clergy as the pre-Henrician church. The Appellants were obsessed with the idea of hierarchical order, as befitted those who saw themselves in the tradition of the medieval church. They rejected many of the innovations of the Counter Reformation, especially the widening of the religious ideal epitomised by the Jesuits. The Appellants believed that religious orders should remain in the cloister and that worldly business in the church should be left to seculars. The Appellants' stress on hierarchy was not merely a conservative stance, but was linked to the desire for toleration. Earlier than the Jesuits, the Appellants were prepared to see catholicism as a tolerated minority religion, which was the only condition under which episcopacy would be possible. But they accepted that in return for toleration the Elizabethan government must be offered the disciplined loyalty of catholics, which would only be possible if the church was hierarchically ordered. As far as the Jesuits were concerned, their reputation ran counter to the ideal of toleration until after 1603, when they came to accept that catholicism could achieve nothing more than sectarian status in England.

Despite internal conflicts among the seminary priests, the number of committed catholics was expanding by the end of the Elizabethan period. English catholicism did not die the quiet death that Elizabeth had hoped for and as some modern historians have asserted, despite losses in Cumberland and north Wales. Perhaps, as the Jesuit Henry Tichbourne believed, the dynamism of catholicism was a heroic reaction to Elizabethan persecution. In 1592 he wrote: 'It is marvellous that the rigours of the laws, and the severe executions thereof these 10 or 12 years have been the foundation of our credit and an inducement to men to adventure their skin and bone for God's sake and the saving of souls' (**1**).

Tichbourne was probably right, but not for the reasons he imagined. By 1603 the rigours of Elizabethan government policy had eliminated catholicism within the Elizabethan church, so that catholicism was now a distinctive, separated religion. This new sect, though numerically smaller than the more widely defined catholicism of the 1560s, was expanding. This was due mainly to the work of the missionary priests, and as their numbers increased so did the number of separated catholics.

3 James I and the Catholics

James I's accession brought a note of optimism to English catholics, for the new King appeared to hold out the promise of some form of toleration. The catholic gentry badly needed respite from persecution and it is significant that it was Thomas Tresham, a recusant, who had paid out more than £2,000 in fines in Elizabeth's reign, who presented a petition to James in 1603 pleading for more lenient treatment for catholics. Toleration was needed not merely to uphold the financial position of the recusant gentry, but also to prevent a further loss of social and political power.

The succession issue, prior to 1603, had divided English catholic opinion, with Parsons advocating support for the Spanish Infanta. But by June 1603 the English College at Rome was celebrating James's accession with a solemn mass, wishing the King 'long life and happy reign' (**84**). Parsons, in a letter to James the following October, claimed that the principal English catholics abroad supported the accession of the new King. Moreover, the majority of the English gentry had always dissented from the Spanish succession; they had instead put their faith in James's granting toleration. James had corresponded with the Earl of Northumberland and doubtless the prospective King agreed with him that 'it were a pity to lose so good a kingdom for not tolerating a mass in a corner'. The answer James gave to the Earl showed his attitude: 'As for the catholics, I will neither persecute any that will be quiet and give but an outward obedience to the law, neither will I spare to advance any of them that will by good service worthily deserve it' (**68**, pp. 148–9).

It is difficult to assess whether James sincerely wished to grant a limited toleration to catholics. He had already offered pledges in 1600 to the English protestants which appeared to rule out such toleration. His agent, James Hamilton, assured protestants that the King would 'not only maintain and continue the profession of the Gospel there, but withal not suffer or permit any other religion to be professed and avowed within the bounds of that kingdom' (**38**). Moreover, James was personally far more inclined to Calvinist doctrine than was Elizabeth. In 1604 James was quoted as saying that 'predestination and election dependeth not upon any qualities, actions or works of man, which be mutable, but upon God, his eternal and immutable decree and purpose' (**96**). But Bishop Bancroft had been negotiating with the Appellants since 1598 (see pp. 37–9), so James's early efforts at toleration were not new.

At first James's policy towards the catholics was favourable. Although he ordered the collection of recusant fines in May 1603 – a decision that helped to precipitate the foolish plot of William Watson – he remitted these in the following July, after representations from the French ambassador. The Jesuit action in betraying William Watson to the King, and James's gratitude to Pope Clement VIII for withholding the threat of excommunication on his accession, may well have been the decisive factors in pushing him towards toleration. The King always held to the ideal of ultimate unity for catholics and protestants in a universal church. James was even prepared to grant the Pope a high place in a united church so long as he would 'but quit his godhead and usurping over kings'. But James's tolerant policy towards the recusants was short-lived; in November 1604 he ordered the levying of fines again (**37**).

The reason for this move is probably to be found in Parliament. The treaty with Spain in 1604, and Bancroft's campaign against puritan ministers, made concessions to catholics very difficult. James, in part, had already recognised this by the proclamation of February 1604 banishing priests. In the summer of 1604 James promised Parliament that he would begin enforcing the penal laws against catholics, probably because of his need for a subsidy and his hope for a union between England and Scotland. The reimposition of recusancy fines was a particular blow to the catholics, since by 1604 the issue of toleration had taken on a new significance. Toleration was the essential counterpart to the Appellants' policy of accepting catholicism as a minority religion and rejecting the tradition of political catholicism hitherto maintained by the Jesuits. When the Jesuits accepted the accession of James, and when Spain, on making peace with England in 1604 (see p. 43), abandoned its policy of supporting rebellious catholic activity there, the catholic body was put in a position where a plea for toleration was the only rational policy.

It has been argued that the Elizabethan persecution of the 1580s forced certain options on the catholic gentry, especially in those areas where persecution was effective. Catholics could try to subvert the Elizabethan state; they could withdraw from all political activity; or they could attempt to continue to participate in the process of government, both local and central (**103**, pp. 149–62). The catholics who attempted to turn their backs on politics either withdrew to their country estates or sought asylum overseas. Many of the East Anglian gentry concentrated on profitable farming and estate management so that, with the help of occasional attendance at Anglican services by the head of the household, they could withstand the financial penalties imposed on them for their catholicism. Other catholics continued to be politically involved. In Worcestershire, for example, there were catholic MPs throughout the Elizabethan period; in 1562–63 Ralph Sheldon represented the county, John Littleton in 1584 and 1586, and Edmund Colles in 1597. In the 1604 election a catholic faction attempted to elect Sir Edward Harewell. The other candidates attempted to keep Harewell and his supporters out of Worcester by placing an armed guard on the gates and Harewell was not elected. This incident was not unique in early seventeenth-century elections, as a report from Durham in November 1603 indicates: 'They [the papists] are already labouring tooth and nail for places in the Parliament, and do so mightily prevail by their importance and indirect means as I cannot see how their dangerous course can be stopped, unless some higher authority speedily interposes itself' (**103**, p. 158).

Despite catholic involvement in the 1604 election, such political activity was not common. In 1604 it was probably occasioned by hopes for a more tolerant policy by James I. The failure in Worcestershire, in fact, might have encouraged more violent action; it is significant that families such as the Littletons and the Habingtons, who had supported Sir Edward Harewell in 1604, figured prominently in the Gunpowder Plot.

The Gunpowder Plot

The Gunpowder Plot was directly linked to James's failure to grant some form of toleration to catholics. The five earliest plotters swore an oath of conspiracy after the proclamation of February 1604, and the digging of the tunnel began after the collection of recusancy fines in November 1604. The origins of the plot, however, go back beyond the issues of 1604. Professor Bossy has seen the plot 'as the last fling of the Elizabethan tradition of a politically engaged catholicism'. He argues that 'one must surely recognize in the mind of Robert Catesby, its moving spirit, a garbled version of political themes which had been enunciated by pro-Spanish catholics during the reign of Elizabeth' (**77**, p. 95).

Professor Bossy's stress on the plot's being in the tradition of the pro-Spanish element in English catholicism has received support in a recent work by Professor Loomie (**90**), while as long ago as 1938 A. H. Dodd stated that the Gunpowder Plot had its origins in the dispute over succession (**84**). A minority of English catholics had hoped for a Spanish succession, and by 1602 the Spanish court was prepared to consider supporting the Infanta with a military force, though the Infanta herself was far from enthusiastic. In February 1603, however, the Spanish Council advised Philip III to support 'a native English candidate'. Nevertheless, the peaceful accession of James I did not end Catholic hopes of Spanish intervention. In June 1603 both Guy Fawkes and John Wright, Robert Catesby's agent, were at the Spanish court. Guy Fawkes tried to convince the Spaniards that revolt was simmering among English catholics and that the hostility between the English and the Scots would produce trouble, regardless of religion [**doc. 10**]. But Philip III's ambassador in London warned his king not to trust the analysis of the pro-Spanish English catholics. 'In matters of importance that hold so many risks, I assure your Majesty that I would not dare to trust these people in this question, although I believe them to be very sincere catholics' (**90**, p. 132). In early 1604, with the prospects of a formal peace between England and Spain, the Spanish Council rejected any thought of intervention, arguing that 'what is necessary for these catholics is that their king does not become suspicious of them at the very moment when the conclusion of the conversations about peace is being awaited' (**90**, p. 133).

Anglo-Spanish peace in 1604 signalled the end of Spanish interest in supporting catholic risings such as that of the Northern Earls or the Throgmorton Plot. Spanish policy from 1604, though still concerned with the fate of English catholics, was radically different from the interventionist policies of the Elizabethan era [**doc. 11**]. The Gunpowder Plot was a violent reaction by a group who had hoped that the problems of the English catholics could be solved by foreign help, only to see all such hopes fade away in the improving relations between England and Spain. Yet despite the fact that the majority of English catholics condemned the Plot, it would be mistaken to dismiss it as the work of fanatics who were totally cut off from the mainstream of English catholicism. The plotters were all second-generation recusants, whose fathers had been knighted. They came from areas of gentry catholicism in the midlands and south-west where the pressure of the government was being felt through the collection of recusancy fines. It was the simultaneous collapse of the Elizabethan Jesuit traditon and the failure to gain toleration under James that, by apparently closing the avenue to peaceful progress, prompted these catholics to violent measures.

REACTIONS TO THE PLOT

The Gunpowder Plot made a profound impression on James. 'The King is in terror,' wrote the Venetian ambassador. 'He does not appear nor does he take his meals in public as usual. He lives in the innermost rooms with only Scotsmen about him. The lords of the Council also are alarmed and confused by the plot itself and by the King's suspicions' (**68**, p. 227). One of James's first reactions was to seek the help of the papacy, and the new relationship between England and Spain enabled the King to try to use Spanish influence. Cecil told the Spanish ambassador immediately after the plot that 'if his Holiness would be pleased to write a very moderate letter . . . pledging that all catholics of this kingdom would be good, loyal subjects, and that he will require this of them under excommunication, and even to take up arms in the King's defence against those who might want to agitate and wage war against this crown, then the King will remit the fines and penalties and allow them to have clergy within their residences so that they might live as they please' (**9**). Rome, of course, could not make such a commitment. Moreover, Anglo-papal relations deteriorated in January 1606, when Pope Paul V succeeded Clement VIII, with whom James had been on good terms ever since his accession. According to the Venetian ambassador, James, in early 1606, made a speech violently denouncing Rome and catholicism.

> I have despatches from Rome informing me that the Pope intends to excommunicate me; the catholics threaten to dethrone me and to take my life unless I grant them liberty of conscience. I shall most certainly be obliged to stain my hands with their blood, though sorely against my will . . . I do not know upon what they found this cursed doctrine that they are permitted to plot against the lives of princes. Sometimes I am amazed when I see that the Princes of Christendom are so blinded that they do not perceive the great injury inflicted on them by so false a doctrine (**68**, p. 227).

The Gunpowder Plot and worsening relations with Rome inevitably led to greater persecution of catholics. F. C. Dietz argues that recusancy fines rose from £2,000 in 1605 to £10,000 in 1606, and although these figures are not necessarily correct it is the case that convictions for recusancy in London and Middlesex were three times higher in 1606 than in the previous year (**5, 32**).

A new session of Parliament in 1606 endorsed the King's harsher policy towards the catholics with 'An Act for the better discovering and repressing of Popish Recusants', which covered a wide range of issues, but made two changes of particular importance. Firstly there was an attempt to tackle the old problem of the Church Papist who refused Anglican communion. The Commons advocated large fines, but the Lords moderated the Commons' demands so that non-communicants were fined only £20 per year. Another change under the statute was the right given to the Crown to take two-thirds of recusants' lands instead of the £260 fine. Previously, land could be taken only if the recusant defaulted on his fine.

Though significant, neither of these new measures had great practical consequences. The clause concerning the taking of land applied only to the minority of recusants paying the full £260, and although one wealthy widow, Jane Shelley, did conform when the Exchequer threatened her land instead of accepting her £260, such cases were rare. The fines for non-communicants were too low to effect significant changes, especially as the enforcement of this clause was left to informers. An accompanying statute of 1606, 'An Act to prevent and avoid dangers which may grow by Popish Recusants', was an attempt to eliminate the loopholes in the Elizabethan penal code. It stipulated that no convicted recusant could come to court without licence, nor practise medicine. Indeed no recusant, or anyone with a recusant wife, could 'exercise any public office in the commonwealth'.

In the main the legislation of 1606 was more important as an expression of Parliament's and the government's anti-catholic sentiment than as a barometer of actual persecution. There is plenty of evidence that many of the measures were ineffective; recusants continued to practise medicine, and John Gee, the anti-catholic propagandist, lists some thirty catholic doctors in London alone in 1624. A number of people in public office had recusant wives, including Henry Spiller, who was in charge of recusant revenue at the Exchequer. The growth of court catholicism under Charles I made a nonsense of this particular legislation.

The most important and troublesome measure for catholics to emerge from 'An Act for the better discovering and repressing of

Popish Recusants' resulted from James's determination to ensure the loyalty of his catholic subjects. The final clause of the statute introduced the Oath of Allegiance [**doc. 12**] 'for the better trial how his Majesty's subjects stand affected in the point of their loyalty and due obedience'. In the Oath of Allegiance, James returned to the central point made on a number of occasions by Robert Cecil in 1605; that the government's treatment of catholics was dependent on their recognising, without equivocation, the temporal power of the English crown. Despite James's violent denunciation of the Gunpowder Plot, he had not abandoned his earlier views. He recognised the conspiracy as the work of a few, and declared that though 'no sect of the heathen, though they worshipped the very Devil, preached the overthrow of governments as did some catholics, yet many catholics were good men and loyal subjects' (**68**, p. 226).

The Oath of Allegiance was of central importance in James's policy towards the recusants over the next few years. Refusal could bring not only its own penalty of *praemunire*, but also the full battery of the penal laws, while the taking of the Oath was frequently accompanied by a milder application of the penal statutes. But between 1606 and 1610 the evidence suggests that James did not administer the Oath or the penal laws as vigorously as he might have done, notwithstanding the increased persecution of 1606 which we have already discussed. The King appears to have recognised that the Oath could raise problems of conscience for catholics, and that pleas against it could be convincing [**doc. 13**]. Moreover, it was not the only test of catholic loyalty. This emerges. clearly in James's instructions to the judges in 1608. 'For recusants the new Oath – the refusal whereof bringeth praemunire – not to be tendered but to apostates and practizers' (i.e. recently converted and activist catholics), while to the rest the judges were to show a 'mild inclination' (**12**). James also instructed the judges that no priest was to be executed who would take the Oath of Allegiance, or who would be willing to listen to protestant persuasion.

Despite James's moderate approach, the Oath of Allegiance proved troublesome to catholics. It raised the question of the Pope's deposing power in an acute form, thus opening up old controversies within the catholic ranks. Robert Parsons immediately concluded that English catholics could not take the Oath, but the Archpriest Blackwell, leader of the secular clergy, initially gave the Oath his approval. Blackwell's action was promptly reproved from Rome by Cardinal Bellarmine, whose 'Disputationes de Controversies adversus huius temporis haereticos', printed between 1586 and 1593, had defended the Pope's right to depose heretical or protestant princes.

With Rome firmly opposed to any catholic taking the Oath, English recusants were placed in an unenviable position. An anonymous catholic letter-writer complained that of the many crosses they had to bear, none was so burdensome as the Oath of Allegiance. Some catholics took the Oath, but others refused, feeling obliged to 'submit themselves to the ruling of the Pope, who had declared the Oath unlawful'. Typical of the catholic stance was the statement that 'the faithful do not want to be lacking in due allegiance to the King, yet are troubled in conscience' (**14**) [**doc. 13**].

When Rome and Cardinal Bellarmine denounced the Oath of Allegiance, James felt obliged to reply, which he did with his *Apology*, published in 1608. In the *Apology* he contrasts the horrors of the Powder Plot with his early clemency towards catholics, and he constantly reiterates the point that the new Oath is a matter of civil obedience, which impinges on no article of faith or spiritual subject. The Oath, James argued, was meant merely to separate his loyal subjects from traitors. As for Bellarmine's contention that it sprang from a groundless fear on James's part of assassination plots inspired by Rome, James quoted the case of the murder of the French king, Henry III, and the many attempts against Elizabeth. As the *Apology* progresses, its tone becomes more aggressive; before the end of the work, James descends to calling Bellarmine 'a liar and a madman'. In 1609 James decided to publish his *Apology*, with a dedication to all christian kings and princes. Copies of the work were forwarded to foreign courts, but even Henry IV of France, who might have been expected to endorse James's sentiments, received his copy only 'with civility'. The Venetians refused to publish James's work, despite vigorous protests from the English ambassador, Sir Henry Wootton. James had fared badly in his exchanges with Rome; indeed one writer describes the whole affair as highly damaging. 'It was in such petty and miserable squabbles that James compromised his own dignity and the honour of England, before the eyes of all princes in Europe' (**68**).

Increased persecution

By 1610 a number of factors were combining to persuade James towards greater persecution of catholics. The fourth session of the 1604 Parliament, which met in February 1610, called for a stricter

Descriptive Analysis

application of the penal laws and in particular a more stringent administration of the Oath of Allegiance. The need for such an Oath was apparently reinforced while Parliament was in session with news of the assassination of Henry IV of France, an event which 'gave a shock to the whole English nation'. In England the 'Jesuits incurred violent suspicion' as the instigators of Henry IV's murder and the 'House of Commons eagerly approved the opportunity to urge a fresh expulsion of all the individuals of that order from England, and a revival of the severities against recusants'. In his reply to Parliament James admitted that the penal laws could be enforced more strictly, but he argued somewhat dubiously that he 'must blame both the judges and you, my lords of the clergy, that the laws are not executed upon papists... . Take care this Parliament that the papists be from time to time strictly presented and according to the statutes already made and duly published.' Nevertheless James implicitly defended his policy of distinguishing between different sorts of catholics. 'I have noted two kinds of papists in this kingdom, the one ancient the other apostates, who shall never have my favour or good looks... . For the ancient papists there is divers of them so honest and fair-conditioned men as if I were a subject I could be content to live and spend my time with them.' (**12**)

The consequences of greater persecution after 1610 were felt especially on the issue of the Oath of Allegiance. Writing in September 1611 a catholic priest lamented that he 'left in England a great persecution of the catholic laity over the Oath. Except for my Lord [probably Lord Montague] and his people I hear that few have refused it.' But not all recusants submitted, and by 1613 there were some forty recusants and eleven priests in the London prisons alone for refusing the Oath, while reports allege that sixty poor recusants were imprisoned in York for the same offence. Some indication of the problem the Oath posed for catholics can be seen from the sums which richer people were ready to pay in order to secure their immunity: William Middleton of Yorkshire offered £400 and said that he was willing to give temporal obedience to the King, but could not take the Oath because part of it 'remained obscure to his unlearned mind'. Henry James, a very prominent Kentish recusant, begged the King to accept a sum instead of taking the Oath; he offered as much as 'my estate may beare, so my selfe and my children may be able to live and be preserved from ruyne and overthrowe'.

A change in ecclesiastical leadership contributed further to the

48

sufferings of catholics. The appointment of George Abbot as Archbishop of Canterbury in 1611 drew a sharp reaction from the catholic population, one of whom described the new Archbishop as 'a brutal and fierce man and a sworn enemy of the very name of catholic'. A Jesuit writing in 1611 saw the appointment of Abbot as a sure sign that the King 'meditates the extermination of all catholics'. The same writer contended, with reference to the persecution in 1611, that 'the times of Elizabeth, although most cruel, were the mildest and happiest in comparison with those of James' (**14**). The appointment of Abbot may in itself have been a reflection of James's religious policy in 1611. An Abbot letter, probably of 1612, to Archbishop Matthew of York, says that the King had instructed the Council and the judges to 'rid his kingdom of popish recusants'. In this changed climate the Lord Mayor of London seized the opportunity for persecution when in November 1612 he wrote eagerly to Abbot of how he was going to enforce more strictly the penal laws against catholics 'out of zeal for religion and the better safety of the King's person'.

In the years between 1610 and 1613 foreign affairs, and in particular England's relations with Spain, were an important element in shaping domestic policy. In 1610 England drew close to the anti-Habsburg powers, led by France, over the Jülich-Cleves crisis. The proposed anti-Habsburg coalition collapsed with the death of Henry IV, but by 1612 marriage articles had been signed between James's daughter Elizabeth and the calvinist Frederick of the Palatinate. Relations between England and Spain, which looked more promising after the death of Henry IV, deteriorated again in 1611 when James, opening marriage negotiations for a Spanish bride for his son Henry, was offered only a younger daughter. By 1613 England had a defensive alliance with the German protestant princes.

The arrival in August 1613 of Diego Sarmiento de Acuña, better known as Count Gondomar, as Spanish ambassador in London, signalled a closer relationship between England and Spain. The severity of the persecution appears to have lessened after 1613, and there are fewer complaints from the catholics. But the moderating of the severities of 1610–13 should not be overemphasised. Gondomar, in an early report to Philip III, stressed the continued persecution of catholics, especially over the Oath of Allegiance. 'Out of this Oath', he said, 'stems the increased persecution of the catholics of this kingdom.' Writing again in May 1614, Gondomar warned Philip not to be misled by James's stance of 'not appearing to be very severe against catholics'. For reasons of state the English king gave this impression, whereas the laws against catholics were generally 'the most severe that they have ever been in any persecution that the church has suffered' (**9**, vol. 2, p. 31). Between 1613 and 1621, when James responded to a very critical Parliament by temporarily increasing persecution again, the vigour of the King's anti-catholic policy fluctuated, partly in response to relations with Spain, and partly at the personal whim of James. Gondomar wrote in 1614 that moderation 'depends completely on the King's good will, in which I am beginning to have less confidence every day, after making considerable efforts to understand it' (**90**). But in discussing the fluctuations in royal policy, it must be stressed that these were concerned only with certain areas of the penal laws such as the Oath of Allegiance, the activities of the ecclesiastical authorities, and the freedom given to pursuivants. Pursuivants were a kind of 'ad hoc' police force, who were commissioned either by the Privy Council or the ecclesiastical authorities. Their commissions were frequently wide and consequently offered scope for great abuse. What fluctuated little during these years were the fiscal penalties against recusants; fines and sequestrations continued practically unabated until 1622 or 1623, when the imminence of the Spanish marriage influenced James to moderate the penal laws.

There was, in fact, a very close scrutiny of the operation of recusancy fines in 1612 and 1615 as part of a general survey of royal revenue. Two commissions, appointed in 1612 and 1615 respectively, called for a tougher administration of the fiscal laws and condemned the practice of recusants receiving the leases of their sequestrated lands. But a minority view also emerged from these commissions, which urged the King to adopt a more moderate policy of greater realism. Long-standing debts should be compounded (that is, the crown should accept a lower sum than the one owed), while recusants should be granted the leases of their lands to encourage greater co-operation from them. If the King insisted on his every due, then 'the recusants simply flee their homes and lurk in secret places'. Moreover, if the administration of recusancy fines was too severe, the richer catholics would conform, so that 'no benefit will accrue to the King'. This, in fact, appears to have happened in 1615, when a drive to exact more money from recusants resulted in an unusually high number of catholics conforming.

James was not impressed by the arguments favouring composition, though Charles I's policy worked along these lines. But the argument underlines the importance of finance in James's religious policy; for by 1614 the Exchequer was annually receiving some

£8,000 in revenue from recusants. Even this figure underestimates their real financial value, for in many cases only a third of the payments made by a recusant went to the Exchequer; the other two-thirds went to a 'farmer', usually a member of the royal household. Moreover, catholics who appeared to have escaped the penal laws frequently paid for their immunity. Gondomar quotes the case of Viscount Haddington, a Gentleman of the Royal Bedchamber, who turned down an offer of £300 from the catholic Sir William Roper of Kent, demanding that Roper should pay £400 to avoid any persecution under the penal laws.

Hopes for toleration

Closer relationships with Spain, especially after 1618, raised catholic hopes of toleration, but little was achieved before 1622. The 1621 Parliament was predictably anti-catholic in sentiment. Catholics, it was argued, must be punished not because of their religion, but because they were seditious. The Commons asked for the full enforcement of the anti-catholic laws, for war with Spain, and for a protestant marriage for Prince Charles. Parliament requested the enforcement of the penal laws almost as though royal policy was one of complete toleration, which we have seen was not the case. Nevertheless, James responded by harassing catholics in London. The Lord Mayor of London was instructed to order his aldermen in the King's name and by his express command 'to search for and list papists in the capital as a prelude to further action'. A fortnight later, in March 1621, the Venetian ambassador reported that the King had issued orders stating that all catholics should leave London for the duration of Parliament.

The dissolution of Parliament in January 1622, leaving James more dependent on Spanish goodwill, lent a greater urgency to the Spanish marriage negotiations, draft articles of which had been drawn up as early as 1615. As a sign of his good faith, in August 1622 James ordered the release of recusants from prison, even if their offence included refusing the Oath of Allegiance or distributing catholic books. By December 1622 important secret articles had been agreed in Madrid. By early 1623 the catholics were optimistic that all persecution would soon cease; indeed in July of that year secretary Calvert assured the Spanish that all further persecution of catholics would be restrained. Spain, however, was not satisfied, but by August 1623 James appeared to have conceded her full demand for complete toleration (**37**).

There was, however, still one major question to be settled; what legal device was the King to employ to achieve such toleration? Obviously James could not remove the penal laws, as they were statutory. The Spanish wanted a proclamation, but James was aware that this might provoke a constitutional crisis. The method favoured by James was to offer a royal pardon to catholics, and this was drawn up by September 1623. It seems unlikely that the pardon was ever published, but the catholics were jubilant, the puritans furious, and Abbot thundered that James was 'labouring to set up the most damnable heresy of Rome, the whore of Babylon'. By the end of October 1623, however, after the bizarre visit of Buckingham and Prince Charles to Madrid, the marriage was off; the two returned to England amidst great popular protestant rejoicing.

The breakdown of the Spanish marriage negotiations did not herald an immediate return to persecution; in January 1624 it was rumoured that Abbot wanted to issue new commissions to the pursuivants, but other members of the Council opposed him. The catholic Bishop of Chalcedon wrote early in 1624 that London catholics were untroubled but that there were reports of persecution in the north. Parliament, which met in February 1624, naturally demanded a return to persecution, complaining of the 'mischief done [by catholics] . . . by their unwonted concourse around London, and flocking to mass at Ambassadors' houses . . .' (**1**).

The King responded to parliamentary pressure, but only with the most ritualistic promise to execute the penal laws and by issuing a proclamation against Jesuits and seminary priests. The catholics had feared new legislation, and they interpreted the King's actions as favourable. 'The catholics feel perfectly happy,' wrote the Venetian ambassador, 'and many catholic lords who had already gone away return boldly to the city' (**14**).

Soon English diplomacy was engaged on another marriage involving religious concessions – this time with France. By August 1624 the King had instructed the judges not to convict any recusants. The negotiations with the French were much less troublesome than those with the Spanish; on the issue of toleration for English catholics they were far less scrupulous than Spain. The French did not try to insist on James's issuing a proclamation announcing toleration, nor even on his granting a pardon to catholics; they would be satisfied as long as no new convictions were made. Even this concession was not fully implemented outside areas such as London and the south where the French ambassador could exercise a personal influence. By the end of James's reign, therefore, catholics largely enjoyed freedom from conviction for their beliefs, but the fate of those already convicted was less certain. This uncertainty was soon answered by Charles I, who, despite the promises included in the marriage treaty, brought back a full return to fiscal persecution in 1626 (see ch. 5).

To summarise James's attitude to English catholics in terms of toleration or persecution is too simplistic. Certain points, however, are clear. Except for a year or so from late 1603 to 1604, the fiscal penalties of recusancy were enforced up to 1623. Recusant lands became an increasingly important source of patronage with which the King rewarded numerous members of the royal household. Other measures of persecution, such as tendering the Oath of Allegiance and commissioning the pursuivants, fluctuated, often quite suddenly. A major factor in determining such fluctuations was undoubtedly foreign policy, but within this broad influence the whim of James himself was decisive. The King wanted to impress upon his catholic subjects that their fate was dependent on him, not on Spain nor on the influence of Count Gondomar. It is typical of the King's policy that he should oppose Bacon's plea for greater toleration in 1617, but that he should also make a gesture to the departing Gondomar in 1618 by granting the release of imprisoned priests. There were fewer executions for religion under James than Elizabeth, yet although the priests who came in increasing numbers to England had less to fear than under the previous regime, life for the catholic laity was far from comfortable. Despite their hopes of toleration, both at the beginning of the reign and in the latter years, they were constantly disappointed. They were in fact subjected to a religious policy characterised by its arbitrary quality and uncertainties.

Conclusion

The accommodation with the government which was sought by most catholic laity in 1603 had not been achieved by 1625. It could be argued that this was not so serious for catholicism since the important factors in its preservation were local conditions, which were still favourable in the remoter parts of England where catholicism was strongest. In 1601 Richard Cowlinge wrote of Hyde, in Lancashire, that 'catholics are so numerous that priests can wander through the villages and countryside with utmost freedom' (**106**). In Lancashire in the 1620s the Jesuit John Layton served a large congregation which met in a decorated barn for masses and sermons. In the 1630s Ralph Corby operated on foot around the poor villages of the north-east of England (**106**). But such conditions as these were strictly limited during the seventeenth century. Generally the increased grip of the authorities over the parishes, together with the growth of anti-catholicism, made the catholic population more vulnerable to government policy. Moreover, catholicism was becoming more dependent on the gentry, to whom recusancy fines and land sequestration were always a reality. It is easy to point out that only a minority suffered financially under the penal laws, but by the seventeenth century all the leading recusant gentry in Suffolk, for example, had experienced some form of land sequestration and a similar pattern is found over much of the south-east and the east Midlands. Even in the north, recusancy fines and sequestration of land were hitting the catholic gentry.

The introduction of the Oath of Allegiance by James I had, in some ways, actually increased the problems of establishing a *modus vivendi* between the catholic laity and the Stuart government. It has often been argued that most catholic laymen took the Oath of Allegiance, but the number of laymen who were imprisoned for refusing the Oath, and the fact that Sir Henry James refused the Oath even after becoming a Church Papist rather than a recusant, must cast doubt on this point. Nevertheless the political position of catholicism was changing. The acceptance of minority status for catholicism, even by the Jesuit leadership, led to a greater political quietism. James failed to respond by granting toleration, but the executions and general harassment of priests lessened considerably, despite catholic fears after the appointment of Abbot. This meant that the catholic laity could practise their religion more easily. But there was a financial penalty to pay, at least for the gentry classes, as there was to be even in the more tolerant conditions of Charles I's reign.

4 The Catholic Community in the Seventeenth Century

S. R. Gardiner summarised the catholic body in the early seventeenth century as 'no petty sect to which a contemptuous toleration might be accorded' but 'a very considerable proportion of the community' (**37**, vol. I, p. 231). Gardiner also argued that catholicism was increasing to a degree that represented a threat to English liberties. There is no need to endorse Gardiner's judgement about catholic dangers to find his analysis helpful. It will be argued in this chapter that the separated catholic body was expanding, and though politically quietist, it was developing into a vigorous minority community.

The theme of this chapter is the change, yet the continuity, within the catholic community of the early seventeenth century, from the early Elizabethan period when the 'old faith' was almost identifiable with adherence to medieval religious practice. Continuity and change can be seen in the social structure, the geographical distribution and the religious observances of the catholic community. The main instruments of change were the missionary priests, who brought a Counter Reformation piety to catholicism in England, but change also followed from the very process of catholics separating themselves from the Established Church. In the seventeenth century the mission became more organised, though this served to heighten the tension between the secular clergy and the regulars (especially the Jesuits), renewing a conflict which had already shown itself in the Archpriest Controversy. Significantly, the seventeenth century saw a considerable increase in the number of regulars on the English mission, and the Jesuits were joined by a Benedictine congregation, the Dominicans and the Franciscans. In many respects the regulars, more than the seculars, epitomised Counter Reformation catholicism, though the seculars' demand for a hierarchy was very much in keeping with the Counter Reformation emphasis on the pastoral role of the bishops (**77**).

Contemporary opinion appears to endorse the view that catholicism was on the increase in the early Stuart period, though some historians have argued that catholicism was a spent force by 1603

(**66**). The 1621 Parliament did not think so and one Member of Parliament doubtlessly voiced the fears of the English protestant nation that the 'increase of papists doth threaten the crown'. Another speaker in the same Parliament bemoaned the situation in Lancashire where 'if 100 come out of a church, as many, by way of affront, will come from a mass' and where 'popish pictures are openly made and shewed in the streets'. There now seems little doubt that separated catholicism, in particular, was on the increase in the early seventeenth century. In London and Middlesex, for example, there were approximately double the number of recusants in James's reign that there had been in the years 1581–1603. Even if London can be dismissed as untypical, the North Riding of Yorkshire also showed a continued increase in the first half of the century. In 1603 it had about 1,100 catholics, but the figure had risen to 1,700 by 1620 and to about 1,800 by 1642 (**19**). There was a massive increase in recusancy in Lancashire in the early seventeenth century. In 1598 the diocesan visitation found 498 recusants, but by 1604 the number was over 3,500, though thereafter it remained steady (**40**, p. 269). It is much easier to demonstrate the increase in numbers of recusants, however, than to establish the size of the total catholic population. Certain contemporary estimates were very high; a seminary priest in 1603 thought that 'the third part [of the entire population] were catholicks. Being demanded whom he accounteth catholic, he said that he accounteth none for catholick but such as do refrayne to come to [the Anglican] church' (**51**). This high estimate of catholic strength received support from the Venetian ambassador, who in 1605 was of the opinion that 'the catholics number a half and perhaps more of the population' (**2**).

Venetian ambassadors are frequently shrewd observers of the English religious scene, but such estimates are demonstrably false. Professor Bossy has recently attempted to estimate the number of catholics in England in 1603 by two different methods (**24**, p. 192). Firstly, he has calculated the number of priests on the mission in 1613 to be four hundred, argued that each priest would serve about twenty families, and then assumed that there would be five people to a family. This gives us a figure of some 40,000 catholics. Secondly, he has taken the diocesan census of recusants in 1603, when a general survey was taken over the whole country, which returned a figure of 8,590. By making allowance for non-communicants, Church Papists and government inefficiency, Professor Bossy arrives at a figure of 23,623. Forty per cent is then added for children under sixteen who would not be included in the recusant returns, and this gives a figure of 39,372 (**24**, p. 192). Both methods suggest a figure around forty thousand. Professor Bossy believes that this may be on the generous side, so he opts for a total of between thirty and forty thousand. He then argues that on the eve of the Civil War there had been an increase of perhaps fifty per cent, a figure which is roughly in line with the expansion already noted in the North Riding.

Detailed analyses of local catholic communities already undertaken suggest that Professor Bossy's figures may well be near the mark. Nevertheless the two methods used are both open to serious objection, as he himself acknowledges. Estimating the size of the catholic community by reference to the number of missionary priests in England may seem the safer method, despite the problems of determining how many families were served by a single priest. It is impossible to calculate how many priests had become permanent chaplains by 1603, but in the early Stuart period the trend was certainly accelerating. An increase in household chaplains may not in itself mean a reduction in the number of catholics served by single priests if the household was a focal point of local catholicism; but since an invitation to religious services in a gentry household usually meant an invitation to a meal afterwards, numbers had to be restricted so that 'vulgar papists' did not have open access to gentry houses. Also it seems unlikely that there was a simple ratio between the number of priests and catholics in the early seventeenth century since the geographical distribution of missionary priests and catholic strongholds was not identical. This point is reinforced by the complaints, especially in the north and Wales, that there were insufficient priests to serve the poor. It seems likely, therefore, that priests might serve a varying number of catholics, so that any single multiplier may be wide of the mark.

Calculating overall figures for the catholic body from a single census return presents even greater difficulties. Government inefficiency has to be taken into account, but to convert it into a percentage of the return is problematic. Administrative inefficiency not only varied from place to place, but from year to year, depending on the personnel involved and the particular instructions given by the central government. Similarly there are problems in trying to calculate the number of Church Papists. Church Papists and recusants were not two separate groups within the community (see ch. 2). Most heads of household had their periods of political conformity, making Church Papistry a variable factor in catholicism. These figures need to be used, therefore, with considerable caution.

Social structure

By the seventeenth century there is little evidence of the feudal type of catholicism found in Durham in the 1560s. Nevertheless important individuals could still use their patronage towards sustaining catholicism in a particular area. For example, Lord William Howard, a recent arrival in the north-west, exercised considerable influence in the Border counties. A typical government report complains that 'such as lately bear sway in those places are most of them professed enemies of true (i.e. Protestant) religion, as namely Roger Widdrington Esquire, George Thirwall, the keeper of Harbottle Castle in Riddlesdale, and William Charleton, great bailiff of Tindaile and servant to Lord William Howard, by whose pretensed occasions with those people upon Sabbath days on the forenoon, the most part of the people of all Riddlesdale, if not Tindaile, are kept abroad in the town streets and churchyards all prayer and sermon time' (**7**). Lord William Howard's servants did worse at Bampton in Westmorland one Christmas when they quite ruined the Anglican service [**doc. 14**]. In such areas catholics still held positions of authority [**doc. 14**]; in 1625 a survey of Northumberland lists twelve catholic families, who between them held offices of stewardships, bailiwicks and collectorships.

The development of the mission and the increased persecution of the 1580s made the gentry more dominant in English catholicism. At the height of the Elizabethan persecution the solidarity of household and tenantry was frequently essential for self-preservation. In the late sixteenth and early seventeenth centuries Derbyshire recusancy, for example, can be explained largely in terms of tenants and servants of the leading Derbyshire gentry – the Langfords, the Eyres and the Fitzherberts. The strength and continuity of the catholic landlord can be seen in Lincolnshire, where as late as 1676 a third of the detected recusants in the Kesteven division of the county came from the parish of Irnham, where the Thimelby family had been landlords and recusants for a hundred years. In Little Crosby in Lancashire the Blundells produced a small catholic enclave. 'William Blundell is the lord or owner of one small lordship or manor consisting of forty houses or thereabouts, and there are not ... any other but catholics in it, except peradventure one or two day labourers, which being born in other places, are come to live there for work.' Such control is hardly surprising in an age which frequently considered that landlords exercised the rights of *cuius regio eius religio* on their own lands. 'I look upon every man possessed of a great landed estate', wrote one landlord, 'as a Kind of Petty Prince, in regard to those who live under him' (**24**, pp. 174–5).

However, the catholic community cannot be analysed solely in terms of landlord dominance. Catholic landowners of the midlands and the south were less likely to have catholic tenants than those in the north, though the distinction should not be exaggerated. In part, this may have been due to the fact that a considerable number of catholic landlords in the south were forced by fines into aggressive policies of estate management which created ill-feeling between them and their tenantry. Sir Thomas Tresham, encloser and rack renter, had many quarrels with his tenants, who by 1600 were largely protestant. Sir Henry James, a catholic knight from Kent, could hardly expect religious loyalty from his tenants when he tried to raise rents so steeply when they became due for renewal around 1612. In Essex, on the eve of the Civil War, a number of catholic landlords found themselves under physical attack from their protestant tenants. Of course the reverse was true too – there were areas where catholic farmers worked for protestant landlords.

Generally the work of the missionary priests reinforced the role of the gentry in forming the catholic community; but in certain areas, especially London, the missionary priests formed a catholic body which was largely independent of gentry control. Indeed, by the seventeenth century catholic gentry visiting London were sometimes dependent on a community of 'middling sort of people' for lodgings and protection. London tradesmen such as goldsmiths, brewers and tailors were prominent members of the catholic community (**5**). For example Christopher Neighbour, a tailor from St Martin-in-the-Fields, London, appears to have acted as an important link between London catholics and Queen Henrietta Maria. In 1632 he was said to bring children to the Queen's chapel for baptism. Even in the backward areas of the north-east, some small catholic communities emerged which 'breathed a spirit of independence of landlord power'. Mr Aveling has pointed out in his study of the North Riding that there was a slight decline in gentry involvement in the catholic community during the period 1603–42. 'The gentry remained very heavily affected by catholicism . . . . Yet in the two decades before the Civil War, the period of slackening persecution in everything except fines, a slight decline set in. Catholic congregations in general continued to increase in numbers and size ' (**19**, p. 257). These examples in themselves are not conclusive, but it seems probable that in areas where the missionary priests were not restricted to gentry households, they produced a catholicism of a wide social mix which was not so dependent on the gentry and which developed the earlier popular peasant catholicism of the 1560s and 1570s.

The geography of Stuart catholicism shows the continuity and change characterised by the social structure. In the 1560s traditional religious attitudes were especially noticeable in the more backward and remote parts of England. The identification of catholicism with the more primitive regions continued into the seventeenth century, and Professor Bossy has pointed out the connections between catholicism and the upland areas, especially in the northeast, noting that uplands were not only primitive but also offered greater protection from government officials (**24**). In the 1620s one Northumbrian protestant considered 'papist rogue' and 'highland fellow' equal terms of abuse. Catholicism was strong in the West Riding of Yorkshire, except for the clothing towns, while the mining districts of Derbyshire were conspicuously less catholic than other parts of the county. Geographical factors were, in fact, more crucial than economic ones. Areas of uplands, mosslands and dispersed settlement, which prevented close government, made the Anglican parochial structure ineffective. This left regional vacuums which in many cases, such as those of West Lancashire, Cleveland in north Yorkshire, and Monmouth, were exploited by the missionary priests for catholicism (**105**). But some of the 'dark corners of the land' in Wales and the north-west were never won over to the separated catholic community, despite the activities of the northern mission as late as 1638–39 [**doc. 15**]. Even in the North Riding of Yorkshire, except possibly for Cleveland, catholicism never gained the support achieved by Dissent after 1640 or by the Methodists in the eighteenth century.

Though by the seventeenth century there is still evidence of individual catholic influence in the extreme north-west of England (see p. 58), the lack of missionary priests there had led to a reduction in catholic strength. In the early Elizabethan period Bishop Best of Carlisle complained of the number of masses being said in the Border region and of the protection given by Lord Dacre and the gentry to catholic clergymen deprived after the Elizabethan Settlement. But by 1590 there was already evidence of decline and by 1617 the diocese of Carlisle had a mere eighty recusants (**105**). By contrast, London and its suburbs, in which there were only isolated examples of catholicism before the 1570s, had an expanding recusant body in the first half of the seventeenth century. In East Anglia, too, there seems to have been a steady expansion of recusancy during this time. It is true that there had been a continuous catholicism in the region from the early 1560s, led largely by those who had made up the household and Privy Council of Mary Tudor: Bedingfield, Jerningham, Cornwallis and Hastings were all Marian servants who headed recusant families. But under Jesuit influence in particular, which began with the work of John Gerard, East Anglian catholicism spread beyond the confines of these prominent families.

Notwithstanding the changes just discussed, the continuity in the geographical distribution is the more striking. The preponderance of missionary priests in the south-east of England did not significantly alter the balance of catholic strength. Lancashire had probably more than ten times the number of recusants to be found in Suffolk in the early seventeenth century. Dr Haigh has recently argued that the geography of catholicism at the end of the sixteenth century closely followed the pattern of allegiance to the pre-Reformation Church. Those areas which had provided a large number of recruits for the priesthood and which had shown an attachment to traditional will formulae, were also those of greatest recusant strength in the early seventeenth century (**105**). Neither the Reformation nor the missionary priests had a profound effect on the distribution of catholicism, and a stable pattern continued throughout the seventeenth century and beyond.

Spiritual life and religious observances

A number of religious practices in the catholic community were pre-Reformation. In the pre-Reformation church both fast and feast days had dominated the calendar. About a third of the year was given over to fasting and abstaining from meat, while about a hundred days were feasts. Feast days had great social significance, being also holidays. Not only was this pre-Reformation cycle changed by protestantism in England, moving towards a pattern based on a regular six-day working week with the Sabbath as sacrosanct, but also in Europe the Counter Reformation was modifying the religious year, cutting down the number of both fast and feast days. Missionary priests were frequently critical of the English stress on fasting. Richard Smith, confessor to Lady Montague, observed that even in her sixties, beyond the age for fasting, she did observe 'all the fasts of Lent, the Ember days and whatsoever others were either commanded by the church or introduced by pious custom of the country, to which of her own devotion she added some Wednesdays' (**24**, p. 111; **11**, p. 48). Only with great reluctance did Lady Montague agree to take meat during Lent when she was on her deathbed. Lord Philip Howard also followed a life of great asceticism, with particular emphasis on fast days [**doc. 16**].

The Jesuits who consciously rejected the ascetic tradition of medieval monasticism in favour of Erasmian moderation, were even more critical than the secular priests of pre-Reformation practices. Robert Parsons accused some English Catholics of ignoring the spirit of religion while 'they relied on such external practices as living on bread and water on Fridays, vigils and most of Lent and things like that' (**24**, p. 111). Jasper Heywood, another Jesuit, shocked East Anglian catholics by his harsh words on fasting. But despite the criticisms of the clergy, the pre-Reformation practice of fast and feast appears to have been common in the catholic community until the Civil War.

If the clergy found the fasting of the English laity excessive, the regulars in particular thought the celebration of the feasts, especially Christmas, too boisterous. But it was a secular priest, Lawrence Vaux, in his *A Catechism of Christian Doctrine*, who issued an early warning. 'If we mispende the holy day in unthrifty games, as cardes and dise for covetousness ... or if we use daunsing for wantonness .... we break the holy day and so offende God' (**13**, p. 33). Despite such words, the traditional folk Christmas appears to have held sway in the early seventeenth century. A traditional form of Christmas entertainment sparked off the controversy between seculars and Jesuits at Wisbech Prison in 1594, when the Jesuits objected to Morris Dancing at their Christmas dinner. William Blundell wrote two plays and a jig for different Christmas jovialities, but by about the middle of the seventeenth century he began to express remorse at earlier Christmas merrymaking. By the end of the century Christmas at the Blundell home appears to have become a sober affair.

Despite the continuation of medieval christian practices, the spirit of the Catholic Reformation was also evident. Mrs Dorothy Lawson, a Northumbrian catholic, showed Jesuit influence in her frequent communions and in a preference for spiritual works of the *Devotio Moderna* such as Thomas a Kempis's *Imitation of Christ*. She was a conscientious follower of the Jesuits' *Spiritual Exercises*, as her biographer reveals: 'Her method of prayer was that which is usually observed in the Society; the matter, the life of our Saviour, taken from points answering to the times of the year.' The Lawson household was one of intense spirituality, typified by the Christmas preparations when 'shee spente the eve of this festivity from eight all night till two in the morning in prayer; littanies began punctually at eight; immediately after confessions which, with a sermon, lasted till twelve; att twelve were celebrated three masses' (**10**, pp. 38–40).

Though the Jesuit influence was evident in the Lawson household, the domestic piety of which it was a model was not necessarily new. As early as 1533 Richard Whitford's *Work for Householders* met a growing demand for books suited to household religion. New works such as Robert Parsons' *Christian Directory* and translations of Luis de Granada were popular in catholic circles, but many Elizabethan catholics at least still used traditional primers. Moreover, the impact of the Counter Reformation was restricted to gentry catholicism, since it was dependent on literacy and regular access to a priest. Here the Tridentine ideal of frequent confession and communion could be followed. In the more remote areas contact with a priest might be irregular even in gentry households, where catholics might be distinguished still by their adherence to fasting and feasting. For the catholic peasantry religion was certainly traditional rather than Tridentine; it meant the mass, Latin prayers learnt by rote, protective magic and pilgrimage (**105**).

Mass, the central catholic worship, provided the greatest continuity between pre-Reformation and later catholicism. But even here there were changes, for only in a few places such as the Welsh borders could mass be said in a chapel. Mass became a domestic, rather than a public, act of worship. Many of the early missionary priests said mass in the attics where they stayed 'like sparrows upon the housetop'. The nature of the household mass is neatly illustrated by the locking of doors at the Babthorpes' house at Osgodby in Yorkshire in 1620. 'On the Sundays we locked the doors and all came to mass, had our sermons, catechisms and spiritual lessons' (**24**, p. 128).

The English mission

Three outstanding changes occurred in the catholic mission between the death of Elizabeth and the outbreak of the Civil War. Firstly, the mission became more organised, both among the secular and the regular clergy. Secondly, there was a large increase in the number of clergy on the mission, especially among the regulars.

Thirdly, there were fierce rifts within the mission, between the seculars and the regulars, a rift which also involved the catholic gentry (**77, 24, 21**).

Any examination of the English mission in the seventeenth century must begin with the appointment of George Blackwell as Archpriest in 1598. Before this date, as we have seen, the organisation of the mission had devolved entirely upon the Jesuits, in particular upon Henry Garnet, the Jesuit Superior in England (see ch. 2). It was entirely understandable, therefore, that the Archpriest regime was intended to modify Garnet's organisation by devolving authority to members of the secular clergy, but not to change it fundamentally. The organisation given to Blackwell in 1598 of twelve regional assistants chosen from among the secular clergy was similar to the regional organisation already established by Garnet. Blackwell did have the additional advantage of jurisdictional powers which Garnet lacked; he could threaten priests with the withdrawal of missionary faculties if they stepped out of line. The Jesuit and Archpriest regime worked in harness for four years, but in 1602 the seculars developed their own separate administration, leaving the Jesuits to do likewise.

The separation of 1602 inaugurated a period of unprecedented growth of the Jesuit mission. In the early 1590s there were only nine Jesuits in England, but by 1620 there were over a hundred. By 1642 the number had risen to nearer two hundred. This larger body necessitated further administrative changes, and by 1623 there was a separate English Jesuit province under the government of Richard Blount. The province was divided into twelve districts, about half of which had existed in Garnet's days. The Provincial continued to live in or near London, kept in touch with local supervisors and handled the finances. The duties of the local superior were to oversee the physical and spiritual needs of the Jesuits in his district, to place them as the mission required, and to see that they spent a week every year doing their *Spiritual Exercises*. This organisation continued virtually unchanged until the middle of the eighteenth century.

By contrast to the smooth operation of the Jesuit mission, the secular organisation was troublesome. The Archpriest regime lasted until 1623, but before that date its inadequacies had become evident. In practice the Archpriest lacked the status among his seculars enjoyed by a superior among Jesuits, and a number of the Archpriest's assistants were more powerful than the Archpriest himself (**24**). Moreover, the split between Jesuits and regulars caused many local disputes. In these the seculars were more likely to suffer because, as a spy report to the Earl of Salisbury said: 'the Jesuits are all placed in private houses such as are well able to maintain them. These places will receive no priest not especially devoted to the Jesuits.' In fact, the relations between the secular clergy on the one hand, and the Jesuits and the gentry on the other, were vitally influenced by an overriding issue – the desire of the seculars to reintroduce bishops into the English mission.

Under the leadership of the Archpriest George Birkhead, appointed in 1607, the secular clergy made strong representation to Rome for the establishment of bishops. The restoration of a full hierarchy would have included the subordination of the regular clergy to episcopal jurisdiction, something Birkhead argued was essential for the harmony of catholicism in England. In a letter of 1611 to Pope Paul V, the Archpriest complained that the conflict between the regulars and the seculars could only be resolved if he were given greater jurisdiction over the regulars (**14**). Another important issue raised in the same letter was that of alms given by catholics to the mission, which, complained Birkhead, were going to individual priests, especially the religious orders. Since the priests did not have to account to Birkhead for the money 'scarcely anything comes for the general needs of the poor, who cry in vain for bread' (**14**). His solution was that 'the regular and secular priests should be bound by the Pope under paine of excommunication to account to the Archpriest and his assistants for the alms received by them' (**14**). The secular priests continued to pressurise Rome. One of the Archpriest's assistants could not understand why Rome refused their requests, despite 'all the labours and prayers of the secular priests'. Birkhead was protesting again in 1613 that 'unless the better order be taken for the religious [i.e. the regulars] they will be lords of us all' (**14**). But Rome did not yield to these requests until 1623, possibly fearing that the appointment of bishops would be interpreted by the English government as an act of provocation. Moreover, when William Bishop was given the title of Bishop of Chalcedon in 1623, this was not the restoration of the normal regime of bishops that had ended in 1559; this was a kind of halfway house. William Bishop, the vicar apostolic, had full episcopal orders, but lacked 'ordinary jurisdiction'. Nevertheless his position approximated to the normal catholic church order far more closely than the Archpriest regime it superseded (**14, 45**).

William Bishop spent only a few months in England, but before his death he established a new administrative structure for the secular clergy (**24**, pp. 53–4). At the top he set up a dean and chapter, supported at a local level by vicars general, archdeacons and rural deans. The dean and chapter in particular was a concrete expression of continuity with the pre-Reformation church, as the right to elect future bishops was vested in it. It was, however, a top-heavy structure. The chapter consisted of a dean and eighteen canons, while the rest of the hierarchy amounted to some fifty people, all to control about four hundred secular priests.

The new Bishop of Chalcedon immediately turned his attention to the Benedictines, who had established an English congregation in 1619 and numbered about sixty in the 1620s. The Benedictines quickly agreed to accept a position of a loosely supervised autonomy. This may have been a conciliatory gesture by Bishop towards the regulars, but more likely it was an attempt to win the Benedictines' support in the battle against the Jesuits. It was Bishop's successor, Richard Smith, arriving in England in 1623, who took up the fight against the Jesuits.

From the start Smith left no one in doubt about his claims as 'spiritual father and pastor' of all English catholics. The first issue he raised was his claim that according to the decrees of the Council of Trent no priest had the power to hear confession unless he had received the approval of the bishop of the diocese. God, he said, would not forgive the sins of a penitent confessing to a priest not approved by the bishop. Smith probably had in mind the eventual construction of a parochial system controlled by bishops, but in the context of the English mission of the 1620s such a pronouncement could only be interpreted as an attack on the Jesuit confessors. Moreover, this action agitated many of the laity by casting doubts on the validity of their confessors (**24**, p. 54).

The second issue that Smith raised, that of missionary finances, was even more vital. Echoing Birkhead in 1611, Smith was concerned about the way the mission was funded. The giving of alms to individual priests encouraged resident chaplains and the concentration of priests in areas of existing catholicism at the expense of the poorer, remoter places. Centralised control of finance would overcome this problem. Smith therefore applied to Propaganda in Rome to authorise such a move, which would enable archdeacons to distribute funds according to local need.

Up to 1627 Smith's main quarrel had been with the Jesuits, but his attempts at controlling missionary finances brought him into conflict with the catholic gentry. Smith subsequently clarified his position on finance; he wished to oversee the bequests left to the

English mission. Though strictly in accordance with the decrees of the Council of Trent, this demand was totally impractical in England. Bequests made by catholics had to be secretive [**doc. 17**), often involving complicated legal trusts. A number of leading catholic gentry, worried by Smith's actions, asked him if he was claiming 'as much authority over the catholic laity of England and Scotland as the ordinaries of old exercised when the catholic religion was established here, and as much as they now possess in catholic countries'. Behind that question lay a greater fear; did the new bishops therefore intend to establish church courts as of old to supervise wills, matrimonial issues and the like? Since most of the catholic gentry had worked out a delicate *modus vivendi* with the courts of the Established Church on such matters, this action could spell disaster. The gentry leaders warned Smith to expect trouble if he pursued this line.

Smith's reply that he was claiming 'jurisdiction in all cases which cannot be brought before a heretical tribunal [i.e. an Anglican church court] either because of scandal or because they involve a priest', did not comfort the catholic gentry (**24**, p. 57). In 1628 their leaders decided to use the English government to rid them of the unwanted bishop. A petition was sent to the Privy Council declaring that recognition of Smith's jurisdiction was contrary to their allegiance to the English monarchy. Charles I replied with a Proclamation in December 1628 for the arrest of Smith for high treason. This was enough to persuade Smith to take refuge with the French ambassador and in 1631 he left England under a cloud (**45**, p. 370; **24**, p. 59).

Gentry opposition to Richard Smith went deeper than the conflict over bequests, or even church courts, vital though these issues were. The majority of the gentry were opposed to the whole idea of ecclesiastical restoration involving a regime of bishops and parochial organisation. The seigneurial nature of the mission in England suited the laity. In such an organisation there was little danger of clerical domination, especially since the more powerful gentry could choose their own priests as permanent chaplains. This was a right that few English gentry, either catholic or protestant, would relinquish lightly.

The Jesuits, as we have seen, expanded rapidly in the seventeenth century, acquiring a position of great importance in English catholicism. A change of Jesuit politics brought fuller accommodation with the English gentry; after 1603 even Robert Parsons, hitherto the most powerful exponent of restoring English catholicism by foreign intervention, recognised the impossibility of such an enterprise (**77**; see ch. 3, pp. 40–41). By the seventeenth century the Jesuits had begun to accept that catholicism was destined to be a minority religion in England. The bond between the catholic laity and the Jesuits was further strengthened by the increasing resort of gentry children to the Jesuit school at St Omer, while more Jesuits were being established as private chaplains.

The Benedictines, from the beginning, stressed the non-political nature of the English mission. William Gifford, an eminent Benedictine, earlier a rebel seminary priest, was a vigorous opponent of Robert Parsons and Jesuit politics. In common with some of the Benedictines, Gifford looked to France as the leader of the Counter Reformation, rejecting the catholic imperialism of the Habsburgs. Another Benedictine, Thomas Preston, denounced aggressive political catholicism, denying even the Pope's right to issue political directives binding on catholics. Leander Jones, an Anglican before joining the Benedictines, went even further by advocating discussions with the Anglicans on the possibility of reunion. As Mr Aveling remarks: 'his ecumenism did not go very far, but at least he suggested that there was much more common ground than Rome and the Jesuits thought' (**21**, p. 82).

The most distinctive contribution of the Benedictines to seventeenth-century catholicism was their stress on the contemplative life. Through the *Memorials* of the Benedictine David Augustine Baker, we can trace aspects of the spiritual development of a contemplative. Baker, an Anglican convert with wide-ranging intellectual interests, launched himself in 1619 on an intense programme of prayer and reflection. During this exercise he experienced physical change. 'Palpitations, great weariness, icy coldness of the upper part of his body and intense heat in the lower part [and] various pains. With them went an exalted state of mind which seemed to bring heightened awareness of God and answers to difficulties.' After this date, according to his own testimony, Augustine Baker never again had a bout of 'serious aridity'. Throughout his life he maintained a high level of spirituality by three hours of prayers every day – one hour in the morning, one in the evening and one late at night (**21, 77**).

Baker did not expect all catholics, priests or laity, to achieve his own level of contemplative religion. But like the Capuchin Benet Canfield, he did believe that all were called to contemplative prayer, and that the best role for the Benedictines on the English mission would be the teaching of the techniques of contemplation.

This, he believed, would achieve far more than the active proselytising of the Jesuits, for the example of prayer would convert many protestants to catholicism.

It is difficult to summarise the development of catholicism in the early Stuart period, a time when the community was 'shaken and strengthened by an intense religious revival bred out of doubt and self searching' (**21**). It is clear that English catholicism was still shaped to a great extent by the gentry, despite the expansion of the mission. After 1605 the catholic body lacked the political involvement which had characterised some of its members in the Elizabethan period. Gentry dominance ensured that remnants of pre-Reformation christianity, especially adherence to fast and feast days, continued, but the catholic community was also part of Counter Reformation catholicism. Even though the term 'Counter Reformation catholicism' cannot be easily summarised, it is clear that the clergy on the English mission, both secular and regular, reflected aspects of it. The Jesuits brought their own blend of the active and contemplative, which characterised the best of sixteenth-century catholicism, and they gave English catholicism not only a commitment to vigorous evangelising, but also the *Spiritual Exercises*. The Benedictines, with their more exclusive stress on the contemplative, represented a very important strand of Counter Reformation spirituality, suggesting links with the mystical tradition already powerful in the sixteenth century. It is tempting to see the secular priests as reactionaries in these developments. But that would be taking too much account of the Jesuit version of English catholicism. Many of the seculars, in fact, had similar aims and led a similar life to that of the Jesuits on the mission. Moreover, it has been argued that the hallmark of the Counter Reformation was its stress on parochial organisation, so that in demanding the establishment of a hierarchical structure for English catholicism, the seculars were in keeping with the spirit of the Counter Reformation. Many of the claims put forward by Richard Smith were based on the decrees of Trent, and in Thomas White the seculars produced perhaps the most progressive intellectual in seventeenth-century catholicism. The seculars cannot be seen purely as conservatives. In summary, perhaps, we can do no better than borrow the words of Professor Bossy and conclude that 'we cannot simply regard post-Reformation English catholicism, in practice, as a continuation of medieval English christianity; on the other hand, we evidently cannot regard it as something totally different' (**24**, p. 147).

5   The Catholics in Caroline England

Charles I and the catholics

'I do indeed observe', said Lord Cottington, Charles I's Chancellor of the Exchequer, 'a great alteration in the enemies of the Church of Rome. Formerly the word Rome could not be pronounced without horror and detestation but now we are grown more mannerly' (**1**). A more 'mannerly' or lenient attitude to catholics has traditionally been seen as the keynote of Charles I's religious policy. This traditional interpretation contains a good deal of truth, but also needs considerable modification. The early seventeenth century, and more especially the reign of Charles I, saw a growing divergence between the court, with its ostentation, sophistication and Italianate culture, and the puritanism of the country, a country that was becoming more critical of mixed dancing, 'those frisks of lightness and vanity', cosmetics and long hair. Recent works on the English civil war have argued that the increasing isolation of the court played a major role in alienating the political nation between 1629 and 1640 (**95**).

A point that is less frequently made by historians is that the isolation and aloofness of Charles I's court is also apparent in the King's dealings with his catholic subjects. While at court catholicism was openly tolerated on an unprecedented scale, the majority of catholics in the country continued to be subjected to fiscal penalties, frequently worse than in earlier reigns. It is true that only three catholics were executed during the reign, a point of no small significance. Moreover, the 'country' catholics probably had greater access to court than during any previous reign: they were allowed to petition for the expulsion of Richard Smith, for instance, and catholic complaints against pursuivants were readily received by the monarch (**1**). It might be argued that Charles was lenient in all but the financial aspects of his policy, and that the fining of catholics was a necessity given the precarious state of Stuart finances. Charles of course did need the money, but the fiscal penalties of recusancy, although the major burden borne by the catholic community, were not the only ones. The King in fact showed little sympathy for his catholic subjects; his vision of catholicism appears to have extended little beyond the court. Charles was attracted to the cultural ambience of catholicism; he aimed to please his Queen and he enjoyed theological discussions with papal agents; but this did not amount to a desire to bring religious toleration to the recusants.

The new reign opened promisingly for catholics. Observing the agreement of his marriage treaty with France, Charles wrote to the Lord Keeper in May 1625, instructing him to suspend all proceedings against recusants. Similar letters were also sent to the ecclesiastical authorities. The catholic body had done its best to persuade the King to grant toleration by pleading its loyalty in the strongest possible terms: 'We believe also and sincerely protest before God and men without any equivocation or mentall reservation that we owe obedience and Allegiance to our Soveraigne Lord King Charles, his heires and successors, and will performe it faithfully to him and them, notwithstanding any Absolution or dispensation to the contrary' (1). In August 1625, however, under pressure from both Parliament and the Privy Council, Charles issued a proclamation ordering the enforcement of all penal laws. Moreover, the Parliament of 1625 passed a new statute increasing penalties for sending children to catholic schools abroad, while recusants were to be double taxed, with poorer recusants subject to a poll tax. In November Charles not only levied the recusancy fines due under the penal statutes; he also ordered recusants to be disarmed, while the Oath of Allegiance was widely administered. The laws against recusants appear to have been operated with greater efficiency than previously; for example some five hundred recusants were convicted in London in the first four years of Charles's reign. Even more significantly the Exchequer showed greater initiative in exacting money from catholics, and between Easter and Michaelmas of 1626 practically every county in England carried out inquisitions into recusants' lands. Where such an inquisition was not the first, the Commission of 1626 generally assessed the land higher than earlier valuations, thus effectively increasing the amount of money paid into the Exchequer either by the recusant or the lessee of the recusant's land. Furthermore Charles decided to reorganise recusant finances within the Exchequer, making a separate recusant account of receipt. The letter establishing the separate department explained that this was done so that the 'said Revenue of the Recusants may be clearly receaved and yt used without the mixture of other monyes and by that means bee more readie for service and maintenance of our Navy' (**5**).

There were certain consolations for catholics. Protection was given to individuals rather more readily than under James I, while the practice of leasing back to the recusant the sequestrated two-thirds of his land was increased after 1626, especially in the north. But such a favour was not granted freely; catholics were expected to pay higher rents to the Exchequer than those paid by former lessees of recusant lands. Another practice used on a wide scale under Charles I, that of compounding with catholics for fines or rentals due for recusancy, was of doubtful benefit to the catholic community. Some individuals compounded for low sums; Henry Foster of Suffolk paid only £16 13s.4d. per year, while Francis Mathews of Dorset paid £12 a year – both generously low for gentlemen. But composition was meant to increase revenue by offering a practical alternative to evasion, thus reducing the administrative costs of collecting fines. In London, where there was a fairly high percentage of landless catholics, money was exacted by composition from recusants who had previously paid nothing, though often convicted for many years. Ferdinand Emerson, for example, a cutler from the parish of St Andrews Holborn, was first convicted in 1602 when he was charged to lose his goods to the value of £5. In fact he paid nothing to the Exchequer until 1628 when he began to pay a composition of £2 a year. As we shall discuss below, the evidence strongly suggests a significant increase in recusancy revenue during Charles's reign.

Despite the renewal of the penal laws and greater Exchequer efficiency, Charles's third Parliament was critical of his religious policy. In 1628 articles drawn up by Eliot, Pym, Sir Thomas Wentworth and John Selden decried the alarming increase in recusants, especially in London. They condemned the practice of allowing catholics to compound for their estates and they accused the Arminians, Bishops Neile and Laud, of preaching popery. The petition demanded the full enforcement of the penal laws. Earlier in the same Parliament complaints were voiced about the freedom catholics enjoyed in embassy chapels, and the Commons asked the King to keep catholics away from London. The King gave the vague promise to Parliament that he would 'keep Religion amongst us free from Innovation and Corruption' (**41**, p. 69).

The year 1628 also saw a significant change in the administration of recusant affairs in the north. Sir Thomas Wentworth, so recently a critic of the court, became head of a new Recusancy Commission, and replaced Lord Scrope as President of the Council of the North. Wentworth had personal views on catholicism; he objected to it because it challenged the established authority which he was now so keen to uphold, and while he was no violent persecutor of catholics, he set rates of composition for recusants in Yorkshire higher than elsewhere in the country. Wentworth's policy of compounding with recusants was heavily criticised by the puritans as being too lenient, but Richard Weston considered Wentworth's policies over-harsh: 'You proceed with extreme Rigour, valuing the Goods and Land of the poorest at the highest Rates, or rather above the value, without which you are not content to make any Composition' (**41**, p. 95). Those less sympathetic to the catholic cause, such as Christopher Wandesford, an officer of the Exchequer, praised Wentworth as a 'light and Comfort to the whole country...for Papists already hang down their Heads like Bulrushes and think themselves like Water spilt on the Ground' (**41**, p. 95). At his trial Wentworth himself claimed that he had increased revenue from recusants within four years from £2,300 to £11,000 per annum – 'more than ever was raised formerly in so short a time' (**87**, p. 212).

The late 1620s and 1630s saw an increasing revenue from recusants, despite the catholic sympathies of Richard Weston, who was Lord Treasurer until 1635. Recusant revenue in Suffolk rose from £103 4s.0d. in 1627/8 to a staggering £728 in 1633/4, though after that date there was a small decline (**87**, p. 214). F. C. Dietz argues that recusant revenue over the whole country rose from £6,396 in 1631 to £32,000 in 1640 (**32**, p. 268; **42**, pp. 91–2). Such figures need to be treated with caution, but the upward trend is clear. Clarendon was certain of Charles's stringent policy. 'The penal laws (those only being excepted which were sanguinary, and even those sometimes let loose) were never more rigidly executed, nor had the crown ever so great a revenue from them, as in his time; nor did they ever pay so dear for the favours and indulgences of his office towards them' (**87**, p. 212).

The financial strain experienced by the catholic community was, of course, in addition to the burdens imposed on the rest of the nation. In Charles I's reign recusants had to pay a double subsidy, and poor recusants an 8d. poll tax. It is hardly surprising, therefore, that catholics sometimes took the lead in opposing Ship Money. In 1636 John Cross of Liverpool, who was described as 'an obstinate recusant', was imprisoned for refusing to pay Ship Money; the sentence probably reflected his past behaviour as a troublemaker. The evidence of personal pressures on the catholic body, already discussed, has led Dr Lindley to conclude that 'Roman Catholics in the reign of Charles I did not experience a period of exceptional leniency and general calm; on the contrary, the reign was a period of great trial for English catholicism. They faced mounting financial pressure from a needy monarch who showed little real interest in their general welfare' (**87**, p. 220).

However, some qualification is needed to Dr Lindley's conclusion. Mr Aveling has described the period from 1627 to 1639 in the North Riding of Yorkshire as one of 'extraordinary relative peace' for the catholics (**19**). Though the financial pressures were great, prosecutions for harbouring recusant servants were greatly reduced and, more importantly, the Oath of Allegiance was rarely imposed. Once a recusant had compounded, there was probably less harassment than formerly by freelance agents trying to exploit the unfortunate position of the recusants. Informers were still employed by the Privy Council, but their activities were more restricted than in James's reign. The catholic recusants suffered great financial persecution, but they were probably subjected less to other forms of persecution and inconvenience. Moreover Charles I's policy towards the catholics was much more consistent than that of his father, a factor which must have brought some comfort to the recusants.

Court catholicism

Court catholicism began in the reign of James I, when a number of Church Papists served the King. Sir George Calvert, a known Church Papist, was secretary of state, while Henry Spiller, receiver of recusant revenue, had himself a recusant wife. William Byrd, Elizabeth's catholic musician, continued in the chapel royal, while his distinguished colleague John Bull became a practising catholic in 1614. There was another sense in which the Caroline court had its antecedents in the court of James I. James's wife, Queen Anne, herself a catholic, was a patron of things Italian, especially the study of the Italian language, and Florio dedicated his Anglo-Italian dictionary to her in a flattering sonnet. The Queen made her children study Italian, and Charles's Italianate interests can perhaps be traced to his mother's influence (**88**). Caroline court catholicism owed much to Henrietta Maria, whose influence over Charles became considerable. But in the early years of the reign

Charles was frequently at loggerheads with his wife over matters of religion; in any case Henrietta Maria played a secondary role to Buckingham in the exercise of political influence and possibly in the affections of the King. England's new Queen refused to witness either the coronation or the opening of Parliament in 1625, after which Henrietta and Charles 'spoke not a word for three days' (**15**).

Charles's failure to grant the toleration agreed under the marriage treaty on the one hand, together with the Queen's ostentatious practice of her religion on the other, kept tension high at court. During the Holy Week of 1626 Henrietta Maria and her ladies lived like cloistered nuns in Somerset House, where a long gallery had been divided into cells for them. The Queen caused something of a scandal by visiting Tyburn, the place of numerous executions of catholics since the 1570s, where she knelt in prayer before the gallows. The London gossip John Pory wrote that the French priests had made 'the pore Queen to walke a foot [some add barefoot] to Tyburn to honour martyrs who had shed their blood in defence of the catholic cause' (**41**, p. 44). The French Oratorian priests in Henrietta Maria's household were in fact a major issue between Charles I and his Queen. In August 1626 the King decided to show his displeasure at the Queen's behaviour by expelling the Oratorians and most of her French courtiers. Charles ordered Buckingham to 'send all the French away...by faire meanes (but strike not long in disputing) other-ways force them away driving them away lyke so manie wyld beastes' (**15**).

By 1627 England was at war with France, with the Duke of Buckingham leading the expedition to help the Huguenots on the island of Ré. But just at this juncture Charles improved his relationship with Henrietta Maria, perhaps because of the absence of Buckingham. Writing to the Duke, Charles enthused that his Queen was 'shoing her selfe so loving to me...upon all occasions that it makes us all wonder and estime her'. After Buckingham's death in 1628 Charles drew even closer to his wife. By 1629 England and France were at peace and Charles allowed the French priests back. This time it was the Capuchins who came to serve Henrietta Maria. 'The Capuchins soon became one of the sights of Town. They were spoken of as strange folk, wearing outlandish clothes and practising austerities that gained many conversions and particularly intrigued the comfortable Londoner, who went to see the Friars as he would to see an Indian or a Muscovite or some savage from the other end of the earth' (**15**, p. 108).

From 1629 Henrietta Maria's influence on court catholicism was considerable, especially after the arrival of papal agents from the mid 1630s. In the area surrounding the court there was an increase in catholicism, spearheaded by a number of French men and women linked to the Queen's household. The Queen's chapel at Somerset House became a focal point for some London catholics, especially after the opening of the new chapel in 1632, an event celebrated by an audience of 2,000 people and bonfires in the gardens of the catholic embassies. Children were brought to the chapel for baptism and a London tailor appears to have acted as a messenger between the London catholics and the chapel in the 1630s (1). But the Queen's influence should not be exaggerated. Charles's desire to placate his wife was doubtless a factor in the developing of court catholicism, but of the crypto-catholics among the leading courtiers more owed their catholic sympathies to earlier contact with Spanish catholicism than to the influence of Henrietta Maria and France.

Some of Charles's leading ministers, especially Sir Richard Weston (Earl of Portland from 1633), Sir Francis Cottington (Lord Cottington), and Sir Francis Windebank have been described by one modern historian as 'catholics under the skin' (15). The puritans certainly thought that a number of the King's ministers were papist at heart. William Prynne, in *The Popish Royall Favourite*, accused Windebank of consorting with priests and Jesuits including 'Francis Smith alias Francis Ryvers...a grande Jesuite, a great seducer and chief agent in the great and damnable plot of the Gunpowder treason'. Windebank in fact remained a staunch Anglican of Laudian principles throughout his life. He favoured the reunion of the English Church with Rome, but he frequently quarrelled with the Jesuits over questions such as clerical celibacy and the communion (15). Despite his Anglicanism Windebank 'spoke like a zealous catholic' according to the Venetian ambassador, and his daughter-in-law became a nun. In 1639 Windebank worked closely with Henrietta Maria to raise money from the catholics for the Bishops' War; eventually he was forced to flee to France to escape indictment by the Long Parliament.

Windebank was more deeply religious than Weston, Lord Treasurer from 1628 to 1635, who likewise remained an Anglican, but whose wife and some of whose children were acknowledged catholics. Weston also permitted his wife to keep resident priests. But despite these obvious catholic sympathies, recusant revenue was on the increase during Weston's treasureship and there is little evidence of favour shown to catholics outside the household circle. Cottington's catholic sympathies also appear to have been limited. He had cordial relations with the leading papal agents to the English court, Leander Jones, Gregorio Panzani and George Conn. But so too did other members of the court, and a recent biographer of Cottington has claimed that the evidence suggests that his ties with the papal agents 'were fostered by the government and undertaken by Cottington in the line of duty' (**42**). Nevertheless Archbishop Laud accused both Weston and Cottington of being too lax with the catholics in the early 1630s, arguing that 'the wisest physicians [Weston and Cottington] do not always hit upon the malady and malignancy of the disease, for now [the recusants] ...think themselves freed from all command' (**42**, p. 121). Moreover Cottington was certainly among the most outspoken of the courtiers who favoured reunion with Rome.

Within Henrietta Maria's household Olive Porter, wife of Endymion Porter, courtier to Charles, was one of the strongest catholic proselytizers. Her husband had embraced catholicism under the influence of Count Olivares in Spain, but in England Endymion conformed to Anglicanism. Olive was converted to Rome by George Conn and thereafter the Porter household was noted for its catholic activities. Charles Louis, of the Palatinate, himself a good Calvinist, warned his brother Prince Rupert not to discuss religion in the Porter household 'for fear some priest or other...may form an ill opinion in him. Besides, Mr Conn doth frequent their home very often for Mrs Porter is a professed Roman Catholic' (**46**, p. 176).

The arrival of the papal agent George Conn in 1636 resulted in a number of court conversions, especially through the influence of the Porter household. In 1636 Sir Kenelm Digby was reconverted, while in 1637 Countess Newport, wife of a puritan lord-in-waiting to the King, also became a catholic. A newsletter of 1638 lamented that 'our Grate Women fall away every day, now 'tis said my Lady Manners is declared a Papist, and also my Lady Katharine Howard, but 'tis love hath been the principall agent in her conversion...' (**21**, p. 128).

The first accredited papal agent in England had been Gregorio Panzani, who arrived in England in December 1634. Panzani was instructed by the Pope to make his primary aim the settling of a dispute between the seculars and the regulars (ch. 4, pp. 64–7). But Panzani was soon deeply involved in political issues with the English councillors. The papal agent had exchanges with Windebank and Cottington, and to the latter he promised that 'if once the

English government would shew itself good humoured to the Roman Catholics, Rome would not be wanting in making a suitable return to them and all other protestant powers' (**15**). But for all his sincerity Panzani was no great diplomat, and in July 1636 George Conn was sent to replace him.

Charles's motives in welcoming such papal agents probably reflected his hope that better relations with Rome might induce the papacy to use its diplomatic power over the issue of the Palatinate. In addition there was a genuine willingness on Charles's part to explore the common ground between England and Rome. Conn found the King not unsympathetic to the catholic church. Charles heartily desired the unity of Christendom, and he objected to the title of 'Supreme Head of the Church' taken by Henry VIII because such a title bred schism. 'I do not admit that I am a schismatic,' the King once remarked to Conn. Charles believed himself to be a catholic in the sense of belonging to the universal body of orthodox christians. 'At the price of my blood, I wish we were united,' said Charles to Conn in 1637, and added that he 'would suffer any corporal penance [to bring this about] but that the Church of Rome was too rigid in certain points especially on the decrees of the Council of Trent'. The King was sympathetic to catholic ritual; he believed in confession as a good moral discipline, and went himself. He had none of the puritan hostility towards the cult of relics (**92**).

Such sentiments did not mean, however, that Charles was prepared to make concrete concessions. The wider issue of toleration for catholics was rarely raised, but even on the narrower point of the Oath of Allegiance Conn made little progress in his attempts to remove a major source of conflict between the recusants and the English state. In December 1636 Conn sent a modified version of the Oath to Rome, in which the catholic subject vowed unconditional fealty to the King and promised to defend him against every enemy at home or abroad, against all invasion, deposition, rebellion, attempted by any prince, priest or people. But Rome objected to the inclusion of the words 'priest' and 'deposition', since they implied a denial of the Pope's deposing powers. Thereafter no further progress was made on the Oath; only on the eve of the Civil War did Charles produce an Oath of Allegiance which catholics were prepared to take when joining the army. Conn remained at court until 1639 but returned to Rome 'soured in mind and sick in body' (**15**, p. 315); he was replaced by Carlo Rossetti, but political events in England soon ended contacts with Rome.

Despite the failure of Conn's diplomatic mission, his influence at court was considerable. As already noted, his arrival signalled a number of court conversions, sufficient to cause alarm among those hostile to catholicism. Contrary to popular puritan opinion, Archbishop Laud was the most prominent opponent of crypto-catholicism. In the Council Laud constantly stressed the perils of catholicism to the Established Church. In October 1637 Laud warned the Privy Council of the dangerous increase in the Roman party; he noted in his diary that 'the Queen [was] acquainted with all I said the very night and highly displeased with me' (**15**). Laud's pressure resulted in three successive anti-catholic proclamations issued by the Privy Council at the end of 1637 and the beginning of 1638 (**41**). These threatened the severest penalties against anyone who heard mass in the Queen's chapel and forbade proselytizing by the catholic priests and laymen (**15**, p. 224). This might appear to signal the end of the more blatant forms of catholicism, but there is no evidence that the proclamations were enforced.

Court catholicism, in the words of Mr Aveling, 'combined menace and fragility in so confusing a way that the soberest observers found it difficult to gauge its real strength' (**21**, p. 132). The central characters played anything but simple roles. Charles's declarations of good offices towards the catholics as expressed to Conn would be more impressive if he had shown any remorse over the harsh fiscal persecution which he had directed against his catholic subjects. By the end of 1637, moreover, as we have seen, the King was prepared to issue anti-catholic proclamations. Henrietta Maria was not an unqualified asset to the catholic community; her narrow superstitious piety was not a particularly good advertisement for the catholic cause. The Queen's household was not above moral reproach; even the papal agents made dismal reports to Rome about the French Capuchins, initially noted for their asceticism, several of whom eventually apostatised. The Porters, whose household was the centre for catholic proselytising from 1636, did not sustain their faith, and all their sons eventually lapsed from catholicism.

The reasons for the significant development of court catholicism are not self-evident. Charles's personal adherence to Laudian principles, which saw the catholic church as part of the true church, doubtless created a more sympathetic environment for the growth of court catholicism, though Laud himself was very critical of this development. Worried protestants had their own interpretation; that, protestantism having failed to bring everyone to the true religion, old superstition was reasserting itself and the court was giving

79

a lead. Part of the reason might be found in the politics of the court in the 1630s, for those who opposed Laud would lean towards crypto-catholicism centred on the undoubted influence of Henrietta Maria. John Donne suggested that the aristocracy, who played an important role on the fringes of court catholicism, were attracted by a reassertion of conservative principle. Any man searching for true religion, said Donne (**21**, p. 140),

> Seekes her at Rome; there because he doth know
> That shee was there a thousand yeares agoe.

The growth of anti-catholicism

'The imputation raised by Parliament upon the King of an intention to bring in or . . . of conniving at and tolerating Popery did make a deep impression upon the people generally,' wrote the historian Clarendon in 1642. 'Their [the Papists'] strength and numbers was then thought so vast within the kingdom . . . that if they should be drawn together and armed under what pretence soever, they might not be willing to submit to the power which raised them, but be able to give the law both to King and Parliament' (**80**, p. 24).

The fear of catholicism on the eve of the Civil War was a powerful factor in English politics, and to this we shall return later. Caroline anti-catholicism had long and complex roots. In the early years of Elizabeth's reign Foxe attempted to link the force of English nationalism to that of the Protestant cause. Writers such as John Aylmer tried to reassure protestant audiences of the inevitability of their ultimate victory. 'Think not that God will suffer you to be foyled at their [i.e. the Pope's and Turks'] handes, for your fall is hys dishonour; if you lose the victory: he must lose the glory,' he wrote in 1559 (**78**). But despite such assurances the nature of English protestantism was often profoundly pessimistic, a point stressed in two recent articles (**78, 98**). The antidote to such pessimism was faith; protestants were exhorted to 'trust . . . in God thoughe the French and Scots and devil himselfe' should conspire against England. But a more immediate and practical solution was also advocated by John Aylmer: Elizabeth should 'cut off the head of Hidra, the Antichrist of Rome, in such sort as it never growe again in this realme of England' (**78**, pp. 113–14).

The doubts and fears of English protestantism were reflected in

Elizabethan anti-catholicism. Elizabethans frequently exaggerated the unity of English catholicism, attributing all hostile actions by catholics to the agency of Rome or the Jesuits rather than to individual English catholics. Typical of this line of thought was the interpretation of the 1569 Revolt of the Northern Earls. As we have seen in chapter 11 the Papal Bull of 1570 arrived *after* the rebellion, yet English commentors were soon asserting that the Bull had been in the possession of the rebels. 'It seemeth by all probabilitie . . . that the originall of this Bull sealed was among our rebelles and . . . kept close among them ready to be published . . .' (**98**, p. 31).

In the early seventeenth century the Gunpowder Plot was seen as the work of the Pope. The Venetian ambassador reported rumours circulating in London that 'this Plot must have its roots high up . . . . There is also grave suspicion that the Pope may be the source of the Plot; as it is a question of religion, it seems impossible that he should not have assented' (**98**, p. 30). The Jesuits, too, were blamed, and the poet Francis Herring wrote (**98**, p. 36):

> Blush, blush (O Jesuites) England knows too well,
> Your counsell furthered most this worke of Hell.

Such assumptions about the role of the Pope and the Jesuits were hardly surprising, for it was this version of English catholicism which the English government stressed. The 'sermons of obedience', for example, asserted that anyone who acknowledged papal jurisdiction was 'freed from all burdens and charges of the commonwealth and obedience towards their prince' by the Pope. Moreover, if popular opinion was wrong on the origins of the Rebellion of the Northern Earls and the Gunpower Plot, the Parsons-Allen line had, until 1603, supported the idea of internal rebellion linked to foreign intervention for the restoration of English catholicism. Belief in the conspiratorial nature of catholicism did not, however, mean that there was a popular or widespread dislike of English catholics; indeed, putting the blame on the Pope or Jesuits was a way of partially exonerating the English recusants.

These assumptions, therefore, did not necessarily lead – as Carol Wiener has argued – to a widespread belief that all English catholics were traitorous, that 'not one good subject breathes amongst them all' (**98**). The evidence of so many communities where recusants lived peacefully with their neighbours, the fact that Oliver Plunket, a known recusant, could hold high office in the Cutlers' Company in London, surely casts doubt on such an interpretation.

James I countered puritan views on English catholics by stating that he reckoned some of his most loyal subjects among the catholic body.

But if Elizabethan and early Stuart anti-catholicism was still limited, it became more powerful and widespread as the seventeenth century progressed. This was due partly to changing ideas within certain groups of English protestants. By the 1620s the very survival of protestantism in Europe appeared to be at stake. In the early years of the Thirty Years' War, Habsburg power threatened to make massive inroads on European protestantism. In this context earlier ideas such as those of the English puritan Brightman, that protestantism would conquer England and Europe over a lengthy period by evangelical efforts, seemed increasingly unconvincing. Some protestants argued that victory for their cause would come suddenly and unexpectedly; Johannes Alsted, for instance, who was professor at Herborn, taught that the millennium was about to be established by a cataclysmic series of events. In England Joseph Mede, a Cambridge theologian, expounded similar ideas. By the 1630s the spread of Arminianism in England had brought the sense of protestant crisis nearer home. Charles I was no protestant saviour in the Foxe tradition, while Archbishop Laud was apparently leading the English Church towards ruin. The puritan writer Sibbes explained why he and his fellows were so opposed to Laud. They were concerned that the Archbishop would set in motion a moral and spiritual decline, the end of which would be catholicism. 'Nothing in Popery [was] so gross but [it] had small beginnings, which being neglected by those that should have watched over, the Church grew at length insufferable' [**doc. 19**] (**80**, p. 36).

Once English protestants felt that they were involved in an imminent life and death struggle, they made their enemy increasingly grotesque. The purity of protestantism was contrasted with popery, which relied on 'crucifixes and Agnus Deis, all for eye, and to snare the heart of a carnall man, bewitching it with so great glistening of the painted harlot'. The Jesuits in particular were seen in diabolical terms by English protestants; they were said to have a 'Mandrake's voice, whose tunes are cries so piercing that the Hearer dies' (**98**). The Jesuit also possessed a poison as venomous as the spider's which would 'infect the hert and stomake' of those around him. By the middle of the seventeenth century William Prynne could even argue that political and religious radicals, such as the Levellers, has been infiltrated by the Jesuits (**56**).

The volume of anti-catholic literature built up in the seventeenth century to produce a stereotype of the papist. But this sometimes violent literature did not produce a mass movement of anti-catholicism as long as there was no political crisis to disturb English security. When such threats did appear, however, they focussed attention on the dangers from catholicism. A rumour in 1596 that the Spanish had captured Calais from the English resulted in a panic in Sussex over a possible catholic rising in the county. In 1610 there were great fears over the number of catholics in London after the assassination of Henry IV in France. When in 1625 England was preparing to go to war for the first time in twenty years there was a widespread rumour of catholic revolt all the way from the south-east coast to the midlands and beyond to the north and west. In the political tension of the 1630s anti-catholic rumours appeared from time to time; for example Bristol was affected by local alarms in 1630 and again in 1636 (**80, 81**).

Neither the development of the grotesque prototype of the papist, nor the readiness of many people to believe rumours of impending catholic mischief, led to overt violence against recusants. The Gunpowder Plot could well have been the occasion for a popular attack on catholics, but no violence followed. Despite the presence of a small but significant catholic community in London, there were few anti-catholic incidents in the capital before 1640. Not even the discovery of a Jesuit 'seminary' in Clerkenwell in 1628 could provoke popular reprisals against London catholics; there were no 'Gordon Riots' in the early seventeenth century. Of course there were outbreaks of violence involving catholics and protestants. In a number of such cases, however, the catholics were the instigators rather than the objects of violent behaviour. In Garstang, Lancashire, in 1600, for example, the Anglican vicar was shot at by a group of 'twenty or more in number armed with javelins, horse staves, guns and bows and arrows'. The vicar had been attacked because he was giving hospitality to a pursuivant who had arrested local catholics.

The reasons for the absence of violence against catholics lie partly in the nature of English catholicism. As a gentry-dominated religion by the seventeenth century, it never severed its links with the protestant establishment, despite the widespread loss of political power. The catholic community turned in on itself for survival, through separate social rituals, education and marriage. But there was also a conformist element which contributed to the close links with local protestants, and there were sufficient marriages to Anglicans to ensure continued relationships with the wider community.

The other reason for the lack of physical violence against catholics lies, conversely, in the nature of anti-catholicism. The production of stereotypes and concentration on the political dangers of catholicism did not necessarily translate itself into distrust of known catholic neighbours. Even in the period after 1640, alarms over catholics were especially common in towns where recusant gentry lived just beyond the urban boundary. Such cases occurred in Colchester, Rye and Newcastle, to name but a few. It was the shadow of catholicism that was feared, the grotesque images built up by anti-catholic literature, rather than immediate recusant neighbours, which produced alarm (**80, 81**). It was the heightening political tension in 1640–42 which translated anti-catholicism from a generalised fear into a major political issue and led to physical attacks on catholics. Alarm over the papists spread on an unprecedented scale; the five major cities in England – London, Norwich, Bristol, Newcastle and York – were declared to be centres of popish conspiracies; so too were many other towns and villages (**80, 81**) [**doc. 18**].

In the Short Parliament, and to an even greater extent the Long, the opponents of the Crown, led by Pym [**doc. 19**], used the fear of catholicism, and in particular the fear that the King might raise a papal army in Ireland, to great political advantage. The parliamentary opposition may have encouraged alarm over popish conspiracies in London, but the countrywide fear of catholicism went beyond this. Parliamentary propaganda was not the sole, nor even the main, cause of anti-catholicism from 1640 to 1642. Even in London the degree of anti-catholic activity went beyond what was useful to the parliamentary opposition. In May 1640 rioters attacked the Queen, her priests, the papal agent and numerous catholic gentry. At about this time there was mutiny and murder among troops commanded by catholics, and two catholic officers were beaten to death in Berkshire and Gloucestershire. By September 1640, with the rebellious Scots in Newcastle, there were rumours of two separate regicide plots by papists in London. Fears receded in the early months of 1641, but they were revived during the crisis of Strafford's execution, when fly sheets were circulating urging an attack on catholic embassies. Catholics were sufficiently alarmed for their own safety to assure Parliament that their religion contained 'nothing to prevent their being faithfull to their prince, and to the liberties of their country, for they utterly abjure that doctrine that the assassination of princes can be justified, or that faith is not to be observed with all sorts of people' (**80**, p. 29).

The Irish Rebellion of September 1641 heightened protestant fears once again, while the raising of armies in August and September of 1642 was a signal for further anti-catholicism. Individual catholics were attacked and hounded; the catholic Lady Rivers had to flee from Gifford Hall to Long Melford near Bury St Edmunds in Suffolk and finally to London. By the end of 1642, however, the worst was over for the catholics, as political crises gave way to fighting.

Part Three: Conclusion

By 1642 the position of English catholics was precarious. In the second half of the seventeenth century it is probable that the numbers in the catholic community began to level out and did not rise again until the eighteenth century. Despite the relative tolerance of Charles I and the growth of court catholicism, no permanent improvement had been achieved for catholics in English society. Quite the reverse had happened. By 1640 anti-catholic feeling had reached an intensity among different social groups which had not been present in early Stuart England.

Many catholics reacted to the outbreak of civil war with uncertainty. Dr Lindley has argued that a significant number tried to remain neutral (**88**), though in a recent article P. R. Newman has pointed out that about a third of the officers in the King's Northern Army were catholic (**93**). Whatever the reaction of the catholics to the Civil War, the subsequent upheavals were a blow to the community. The organisation of the mission was disrupted, while a number of catholics suffered financial hardship. Moreover, the mid seventeenth century saw the formation of a political and social environment which remained hostile to catholicism with varying degrees of intensity until perhaps as late as the nineteenth century.

Whatever disadvantages catholicism experienced from outside, the signs were already present by the mid seventeenth century that the inner dynamism of the community was declining. I am inclined to support Mr Aveling's view that the conflicts between the secular and religious clergy (see ch. 4, pp. 64–7) did not produce such deep divisions in the community as contemporary correspondence might suggest, and that consequently they were not an important factor in limiting the expansion of the mission. But the accommodation between the gentry and the missionary priests did have important results. The greater number of permanent chaplains reduced the mobility of the missionary clergy and while this brought certain favoured elements among the catholic gentry into the mainstream of Counter Reformation religion, it left non-gentry catholics, as well as potential catholics, less well served. This point should not be exaggerated, as evidence from the northern mission in the

1630s shows priests working hard for the non-gentry section of the population. But the success of various protestant sects in the 'dark corners of the land', as previously mentioned, shows that the catholic community had stopped short of its full potential in areas which might otherwise have become strongly recusant. Even in the more tolerant political climate of the Restoration, catholicism failed to expand, and John Miller has remarked that 'by Charles II's reign the English mission was carried on in a minor key' (**56**).

The period 1558–1642 was a decisive one for English catholicism. Adherence to traditional religion was still sufficiently strong in 1558 to justify our talking of a decline in catholicism in the first twenty years of Elizabeth's reign. Moreover, there is some continuity between this type of early Elizabethan catholicism and recusancy; the Marian recusant priests, particularly strong in Lancashire, provided a vital link. The catholicism of the missionary priests was an adaptation of earlier forms of catholicism rather than a new phenomenon.

Nevertheless the changes experienced by English catholicism between 1558 and 1642 were enormous. Catholicism moved from the parish church to the household. In the early days of the new Elizabethan Church, the conformist nature of catholicism, linked to the conservative tendencies of some Anglican priests, kept it close to parochial organisation. But as greater persecution developed and the missionary priests insisted on recusancy, catholicism became a religion of separation. By 1603 catholicism was a minority religion in England.

The exact process by which this minority survived and even grew is not always clear. But the separation had to be accompanied by the development of a missionary organisation in which the social connections of the gentry, the pull of London and the religiously conservative counties, were of great importance. Out of this organisation, a catholic community emerged. In the counties this community was often reflected in the shared religion of tenant and overlord. On a national level the intermarriage between catholics of gentry families, though never exclusive, and the close liaison between the gentry and the clergy, who by the early seventeenth century were fast developing a national organisation, gave the community a national as well as a local existence. But this community, which in 1642 was fast becoming the central scapegoat in national politics, was a far cry from the traditional catholicism to which a good number, probably a majority, of English people had still subscribed in 1558.

Part Four: Documents

document 1
Elizabeth's caution in 1559

*When Elizabeth ascended the throne she approached the religious question
with great caution, as the imperial ambassador noted with approval in March
1559.*

From the very beginning of her reign she has treated all religious
questions with so much caution and incredible prudence that she
seems both to protect the Catholic religion and at the same time
not entirely to condemn or outwardly reject the new Reformation.
... In my opinion, a very prudent action, intended to keep the
adherents of both creeds in subjection, for the less she ruffles them
at the beginning of her reign the more easily she will enthral them
at the end.

Count von Helffstein to the Emperor Ferdinand I, 16 March 1559.
From *Queen Elizabeth I and Some Foreigners*, ed. Victor von Klarwill,
John Lane, the Bodley Head, 1928, p. 47

document 2
Clerical resistance

*Except for the catholic bishops, only a small minority of the Marian clergy
resigned rather than accept the Elizabethan religious settlement. But many
who continued in office showed strong catholic sympathies, as this report by
Bishop Scory, on Hereford Cathedral, indicates.*

HEREFORD CATHEDRAL, 1564
i. Besides mine own knowledge, Mr John Ellis, dean of the said
church, hath certified to me as followeth: that all the canons resi-
dentiary (except Jones, *qui dicit et non facit*, which is rash, hasty and
indiscreet) are but dissemblers and rank Papists. And these have

the rule of the church and of all the ministries and offices of the same and are neither subject to the ordinary jurisdiction, nor of the dean nor of the bishop .... So that they may now do as they like without controlment. They neither observe the Queen's Majesty's injunctions given unto them in her Highness's visitation nor the Archbishop of Canterbury's injunctions given them in his visitation nor yet the injunction of the Queen's Majesty's High Commissioners .... The Communion was not ministered in the Cathedral Church since Easter (as I am informed). The canons will neither preach, read homilies, nor minister the Holy Communion, nor do anything to commend, beautify or set forward this religion, but mutter against it, receive and maintain the enemies of religion. So that this church, which should be the light of all the diocese, is very darkness and an example of contempt of true religion, whom the city and country about follow apace.

John Scory, Bishop of Hereford, to the Privy Council, 1564

From P. Caraman, *The Other Face*, Longman, 1960, p. 43

document 3

Criticism of Elizabeth's policy

Alexander Nowell, Dean of St Paul's, in his opening sermon to the 1563 Parliament, protested that Elizabeth's policy towards the catholics had been too lenient. He argued that clemency should not be shown to supporters of false religion; on the contrary, they should be put to the sword.

The Queen's majesty of her own nature is wholly given to clemency and mercy, as full well appeareth hitherto. For in this realm was never seen a change so quiet; or so long reigning without blood (God be praised for it). Howbeit those which hitherto will not be reformed, but obstinate ... ought otherwise to be used. But now will some say, Oh bloody man! that calleth this the house of right, and now would have it made a house of blood. But the Scripture teacheth us that divers faults ought to be punished by death: and therefore following God's precepts it cannot be accounted cruel. And it is not against this house, but the part thereof, to see justice ministered to them who would abuse clemency. Therefore the goodness of the Queen's majesty's clemency may well and ought now therefore to be changed to justice seeing it will not help. But now to explicate myself, I say if any man keeping his opinion, will, and mind close within himself, and so not open the same, then he ought not to be punished. But when he openeth abroad, then it hurteth, and ought to be cut off. And specially if in any thing it touch the Queen's majesty. For such errors of heresy ought not, as well for God's quarrel as the realm's, to be unlooked into. For clemency ought not to be given to the wolves to kill and devour, as they do the lambs. For which cause it ought to be foreseen; for that the prince shall answer for all that so perish, it lying in her power to redress it. For by the scriptures, murderers, breakers of the holy day, and maintainers of false religion ought to die by the sword.

From William P. Haugaard (**39**, p. 330)

document 4
Edmund Campion on the dangers of the mission in the 1580s

The hazards facing the seminary priests, especially in the early 1580s before the mission became organised, were great, as this letter of Campion, probably written in November 1580, vividly illustrates. The great optimism of the early missionary priests is also evident.

E[dmund] C[ampion] to [Dr Allen?]. Having been here five months, I write to you what has happened since I last wrote from St Omer. I sailed on the day of St John Baptist, my peculiar patron, and my little man [Ralph Emerson?] and I reached Dover early next morning. We were all but taken, for we were brought before the mayor as favourers of the old faith, and dissembling our names; he thought I was Dr Allen, and said he would send us before Council. I prayed to St John, and by his help we escaped, an old man coming forth and telling us we were dismissed; but I believe I shall some day be apprehended.

I came to London to the house where father Robert* was. Young gentlemen came on every hand and embraced me, giving me apparel and weapons, and conveyed me out of the city.

I ride daily in the country, meditating my sermon on horseback, hear confession, and after mass, preach, being greedily heard, and give the sacraments. The country priests are virtuous and learned; they have raised such an opinion of our society that all Catholics

* Robert Parsons

do us exceeding reverence; therefore those who are to be sent should be well trained for the pulpit.

I cannot long escape the heretics, they have so many scouts; I wear ridiculous clothes, often change my name, and so often read news' letters that Campion is taken, that I am without fear. Let those whom you send take into account the solaces that countervail these miseries, and by their sweetness make worldly pains seems nothing, viz., a pure conscience, courage, zeal, a worthy work amongst high and low, in great numbers, even the milder Protestants; it has become a proverb that he must be Catholic who faithfully pays what he owes; and if a Catholic do an injury, it is thought unworthy of his calling. There are no men more corrupt and impure that the ministers, and we may well be indignant that fellows so base and unlearned should overrule the noble wits of the realm.

Threatening edicts come forth against us daily, yet we have escaped thus far; men neglect their own safety to take care of mine. I had set down in writing the causes of my coming; that I was a priest, and wished to teach the gospel and minister the sacraments, asking audience of the Queen and nobility, and professing disputations. I kept one copy in case I fell into the officers' hands, and left the other with a friend, but he did not keep it close; it was greedily read, and my adversaries were mad, answering out of the pulpit that they would dispute, but the Queen would not allow matters already established to be called in question. They call us seditious hypocrites, and even heretics, which is much laughed at. The people are ours, and the spreading this writing has advanced the cause. With a safe conduct, we would go to Court. But they have filled the old prisons with Catholics, make new ones, and affirm that it were better to make a few traitors than that so many souls should be lost.

They brag no more of their martyrs, since now, for a few apostates and cobblers of theirs turned, we have bishops, lords, knights, the old nobility, flower of the youth, noble matrons, and innumerable of the inferior sort either martyred or dying by imprisonment. In the house where I am, there is no talk but of death, flight, prison, or spoil of friends; yet they proceed with courage.

Many new soldiers restored to the church give up their names, whilst the old offer up their blood.

We need much your prayers and sacrifices. There will never want men in England that will take care of their own and others' salvation, nor will this church fail, so long as priests and pastors are found for the sheep. The rumour of present peril causes me to make an end.

From *Calendar of State Papers Domestic Additional* 1580–1625, pp. 24–5

document 5
Increased persecution

Persecution of catholics increased in the 1580s. William Weston gives an exaggerated account of the state of persecution in 1585, but an account which is based on reality. Catholic houses were searched without warning, spies were active, especially in London, and anti-catholic rumours were prevalent. Nevertheless as the account progresses it becomes more exaggerated and by the end it is the kind of propaganda that has coloured our interpretation of Elizabethan catholicism to this day.

IMMEASURABLE SUFFERING

The days that followed the Parliament* were bitter days for Catholics and filled with immeasurable suffering. Earlier, indeed, there had been great cruelty. Many had been broken. But now the fury of the persecution burst upon them more savagely still. It was the power held by the Earl of Leicester that was responsible, combined with Cecil's counsel, for these two men were in control under the Queen. Catholics now saw their own country, the country of their birth, turned into a ruthless and unloving land. All men fastened their hatred on them. They lay in ambush for them, betrayed them, attacked them with violence and without warning. They plundered them at night, confiscated their possessions, drove away their flocks, stole their cattle. Every prison no matter how foul or dark, was made glorious by the noble and great-hearted protestations of saintly confessors, and even martyrs. In the common thoroughfares and crossways watchmen were abruptly posted, so that no traveller could pass peacefully on his way or escape stringent scrutiny. On the same night and at the same hour, now a single town, now several throughout the kingdom, experienced the sudden incursion of secret spies: inns, taverns, lodging-houses, bedchambers, were

* William Weston refers to the Parliament of 1584–5. On 14 December 1584 a bill was introduced 'For the utter extirpation of Popery against Jesuits and others'. It received royal assent on 29 March 1585.

searched with extreme rigour, and any suspected person, unable to give a satisfactory account of himself, was put in prison or under guard until morning; or until he could clear himself before the magistrates of the suspicion that he was a Catholic, and, in particular, a Catholic priest. Untrue reports were set in motion that a hostile Armada was being prepared, even approaching England; counterfeit letters were written, purporting to come from Catholics, disclosing plots against the Queen – it was the fashion to believe they planned the Queen's death. Some spies, in fact, went so far as to disguise themselves as Catholics and get themselves arrested and imprisoned in order to confess their guilt and inflame the people's passion against the Catholics, and so have sharp vengeance demanded on them.

In London sometimes – I witnessed this myself and listened to Catholics groaning and grieving over it – a report would go round and be confirmed as certain fact, that the Queen's Council had passed a decree for the massacre of all Catholics in their houses on this or that night. Then many people would abandon their homes and lodgings and pass the night in the fields; others would hire boats and drift up and down the river. And a rumour was afoot, supposed to come from the lips of Cecil himself, that he was going to take steps to reduce Catholics to such destitution that they would be incapable of helping one another and, like swine, would be grateful if they could find a husk on which to appease their hunger. In fact, it appeared to me that the prophecy of our Saviour was then fulfilled, 'They will put you out of the synagogues: and whosoever killeth you will think that he doth a service to God.'

From William Weston, *Autobiography*, ed. P. Caraman, Longmans, Green and Co., 1955

document 6
Catholicism: the 'Old Faith'

Since protestantism was ultimately successful in sixteenth-century England, it is understandable that we tend to see it as the religious norm as against catholic nonconformity. But for Elizabethan religious conservatives catholicism was the 'old faith', while protestantism was an Edwardian innovation. In 1581 Cecily Stonor put forward this view when rebuked for her recusancy by judges at Oxford.

I was born in such a time when holy mass was in great reverence, and brought up in the same faith. In King Edward's time this reverence was neglected and reproved by such as governed. In Queen Mary's time, it was restored with much applause; and now in this time it pleaseth the state to question them, as now they would do me, who continue in this Catholic profession. The state would have these several changes, which I have seen with mine eyes, good and laudable. Whether it can be so, I refer it to your Lordships' consideration. I hold me still to that wherein I was born and bred; and find nothing taught in it but great virtue and sanctity; and so by the grace of God I will live and die in it.

From H. Clifford, *Life of Jane Dormer, Duchess of Feria,* 1887, pp. 38–9, quoted by C. Haigh (**105**)

document 7
The continuity of catholicism

The seminary priests did not represent a totally new tradition of English catholicism; they were often inheritors of an established English tradition. In a deposition of 1586, Thomas Bramston, a seminary priest, neatly illustrates the continuity of catholicism from the days of Henry VIII to the Elizabethan mission.

Thomas Bramston saith he hath taken no degrees in schools. He saith he was brought up in his young years in the grammar school in Canterbury under old Mr Twine. From Mr Twine he went to Westminster and there continued a year and was a novice in the abbey. From thence he went to Mr Roper of Eltham, where he continued about a year. From thence he went to Oxford to St John's College where he continued about three or four years and was fellow of that college. From thence he went to wait upon Dr Feckenham who was in the Tower, where he continued so about two years. From thence he went to serve Sir Thomas Tresham, to whom he did belong, coming and going, about ten years and was schoolmaster to his house until such time as the Act of Parliament was made that none should teach either publicly or privately but such as would conform themselves to the religion now established, which as he thinketh was about the 18th year of the Queen's Majesty's reign. From Sir Thomas Tresham's service he went over sea, and, confessing that he is a priest, he will not answer to any question, neither when he went over, but saith that he was no priest when he was schoolmaster in Sir Thomas Tresham's house, which was ten or eleven years since.

From H. Foley SJ, *Records of the English Province of the Society of Jesus*, vol. 3, pp. 224–5, quoted in C. Haigh (**105**)

Occasional conformists

document 8

Though the papacy condemned catholics who attended Anglican services as early as 1562, Cardinal Allen, as late as 1592, advised priests to show compassion to those catholics who occasionally attended Anglican services, while stressing that such attendance was unlawful.

1592: Copy of a letter from Cardinal Allen found in Mr Wiseman's house

[Cardinal Allen] Requires those that are priests to use great compassion towards such of the laity as, from mere fear, or to save a wife and family from ruin, are so far only fallen as to come sometimes to [Protestant] churches, or be present at their services; for though it be not lawful nor excusable to do so, yet necessity makes the offence less, and more easy to be absolved. They [the priests] are therefore not to be too hard in receiving them again, and absolving them when they confess and are sorry for their infirmity, and yield hope that hereafter they will stand more strongly, or have means to escape, and not be led into the like temptation. They [the priests] must use this mercy, though they fall more than once, and though there is fear that they will fall again, and no more severity is to be used than in any other sins. Such matters cannot be subject to certain rules, they must use wisdom and charity.... Yet they must have great regard not to teach nor defend that it is lawful to communicate with the Protestants in their prayers, services or conventicles; this is contrary to the practice of the Church in all ages, and of the holy doctors, who never communicated, nor allowed any Catholic to pray with Arians, Donatists, or what other soever; neither is it a positive law of the Church, for so it might be dispensed with upon some occasion; but it is denied by God's eternal law, as has been proved in sundry treatises, and practised from the beginning of their missions.

From *Calendar of State Papers Domestic* 1591–94, p. 292

document 9

The Church Papist

Many catholics, as we saw in the previous document, practised at least occasional conformity. But the Church Papist, the Catholic who regularly attended Anglican services, was the butt of much contemporary abuse for compromising his religious principles.

THE CHURCH PAPIST

A [Church] Papist is one that parts religion between his conscience and his purse and comes to church not to serve God but the King. The fear of the law makes him wear the mark of the Gospel which he useth, not as a means to save his soul, but his charges. He loves Popery well, but he is loth to lose by it, and though he is something scared by the Bulls of Rome, yet he is struck with more terror at the apparitor. Once a month he presents himself at the church to keep off the churchwardens ... kneels with the congregation, but prays by himself and asks God's forgiveness for coming thither. If he is forced to stay out a sermon, he puts his hat over his eyes and frowns out the hour; and when he comes home, he thinks to make amends for his fault by abusing the preacher .... He would make a bad martyr, and a good traveller, for his conscience is so large that he could never wander from it, and in Constaninople would be circumcised with a mental reservation. His wife is more zealous in her devotion and therefore more costly, and he bates her in tires what she stands him in religion.*

From P. Caraman, *The Other Face*, Longman, 1960, pp. 272–3

* Since his wife is a recusant she will be liable to fines by the government and the husband deprives his wife of fine clothes to the tune of what she costs him in fines.

document 10

Guy Fawkes and the Gunpowder Plot

In 1603 Guy Fawkes, hoping to encourage Spain to support a rising against James I, argued that England was ripe for rebellion. This was due, not just because of religious divisions, but also because of the great opposition to the Scots in England.

A holograph memorandum by Guy Fawkes, undated (c. July 1603) from Simancas Archivo General, Sección de Estado 840/126

The peers of England are seen to be unhappy with the Scots mainly for their crudity and particularly for the many quarrels at court. There, a royal page slew a page of the Earl of Northumberland with a dagger. Another Scot struck an Englishman in the Presence Chamber, yet they did not punish him but merely excused him as insane. . . .

Some of the principal gentlemen have not wished to come to the court, although many of their friends have implored them to do so. It is certain if it were not for the fathers of the Society, the schismatics in England would have long since taken up arms . . . because of the slight satisfaction offered to the Catholic religion. A thing which they desire as much, or more, than the catholics, so as to end the war of conscience which kills them by degrees.

There is a natural hostility between the English and the Scots. There has always been one, and at present it keeps increasing through these grievances, so that even were there but one religion in England, nevertheless it will not be possible to reconcile these two nations, as they are, for very long.

A. J. Loomie SJ, 'Guy Fawkes in Spain, the "Spanish Treason" in Spanish Documents' (**90**, p. 63)

document 11

Spain and the English catholics

Ever since 1569 Spain had considered the possibility of intervening to help English catholics. The hope of Spanish intervention had sustained those who had refused to accept that catholicism was a minority religion, including William Allen and Robert Parsons. But with the accession of James I, Spanish policy changed, a change formalised in the peace of 1604. Spain continued to try to help English catholics, but successive ambassadors insisted that they were too weak to form a basis of opposition to James, and that foreign intervention would not be welcome. The Constable of Castile visited London in August 1604 as Ambassador extraordinary to sign the peace treaty. After leaving England he wrote a review of the religious situation in England.

The temporal resources of the Catholics of this kingdom alone are very weak, and they could not and would not dare to attempt anything. While a foreigner's strength might encourage them, it is much more likely after a landing that the interests of other princes would become apparent. They do not want foreigners, especially the Spanish, to come in here, out of fear for their own power.

From Biblioteca Nacional, Madrid, MS 6949 fo. 117v. 22 Nov. 1604: quoted in A. J. Loomie SJ, 'Guy Fawkes in Spain, the "Spanish Treason" in Spanish Documents' (**90**, p. 35)

document 12

The Oath of Allegiance

In the aftermath of the Gunpowder Plot, James I introduced an Oath of Allegiance to try to ensure catholic loyalty to the Crown. Many catholics were keen to prove their devotion to the King, as was demonstrated by previous protestations of loyalty. But the denial of the papal claim to depose princes (clause 3) brought papal denunciation of the Oath. Consequently many Catholics refused to take it.

The tenor of which oath hereafter followeth:

xv. I A. B. do truly and sincerely acknowledge, profess, testify and declare in my conscience before God and the world, That our sovereign lord King JAMES is lawful and rightful King of the realm, and of all other his Majesty's dominions and countries; and that the Pope neither of himself nor by any authority of the church or of Rome, or by any other means with any other, hath any power or authority to depose the King, or to dispose any of his Majesty's kingdoms or dominions, or to authorize any foreign prince to invade or annoy him or his countries, or to discharge any of his subjects of their allegiance and obedience to his Majesty, or to give licence or leave to any of them to bear arms, raise tumults or to offer any violence or hurt to his Majesty's royal person, state or government, or to any of his Majesty's subjects within his Majesty's dominions.

(2) Also I do swear from my heart, That notwithstanding any declaration or sentence of excommunication, or deprivation made or granted, or to be made or granted, by the pope or his successors, or by any authority derived or pretended to be derived from him or his see against the said King, his heirs or successors, or any absolution of the said subjects from their obedience: I will bear faith and true allegiance to his Majesty, his heirs and successors, and him and them will defend to the uttermost of my power, against all conspiracies and attempts whatsoever which shall be made against his or their persons, their crown and dignity, by reason or colour of any such sentence or declaration, or otherwise, and will do my best endeavour to disclose and make known unto his Majesty, his heirs

and successors, all treasons and traiterous conspiracies which I shall know or hear of to be against him or any of them.

(3) And I do further swear, That I do from my heart abhor, detest and abjure, as impious and heretical, this damnable doctrine and position, That princes which be excommunicated or deprived by the Pope, may be deposed or murdered by the subjects, or any other whatsoever.

(4) And I do believe, and in my conscience am resolved, That neither the Pope nor any other person whatsoever, hath power to absolve me of this oath or any part thereof, which I acknowledge by good and full authority to be lawfully ministred unto me, and do renounce all pardons and dispensations to the contrary.

(5) And all these things I do plainly and sincerely acknowledge and swear, according to the express words by me spoken, and according to the plain and common sense and understanding of the same words, without any equivocation or mental evasion, or secret reservation whatsoever: and I do make this recognition and acknowledgement heartily, willingly and truly, upon the true faith of a christian.

So help me God.

Statutes of the Realm Anno tertio Jacobi C.4, 1606

document 13

Catholic refusal of the Oath

Some catholics took the Oath of Allegiance, but more appear to have refused. The reasons for refusal ranged from arguing that the Oath concerned the nature of the Church as well as temporal allegiance, to pleading that the Oath was too complicated for simple men! The account below, probably written in about 1607–8, is typical of documents circulating at the time explaining the reasons why catholics refused to take the Oath.

6 Reasons for refusing the oath

Reasons of refuzall.

1. Yf the late parliament oathe did conteyne nothing but onely matter of temporal allegeaunce to the Kinge's Majestie, his heires and lawfull successors, no true English subjecte, beinge offred the same, but would take it hartelie and willinglie. But beinge a mixte oathe, partlye acknowledginge temporall allegiance, but cheifelie

denyenge the aucthoritie and power of the Churche, which howe farre it reacheth is unknowne (consideringe the ritch endowmentes of power and aucthoritie given thereunto, and to the pastors thereof, by our Savior Christe in holie Scriptures), it is therefore impossible to be trulie lymitted by an othe.

2. Yf anie successor should usurpe the governement of this realme, and should embrace Turkysme or Arranisme, and commaund the same to be professed thoroughe this realme, or should seeke the subvertion of the lawes and state; or yf the two kingdomes of England and Scotland (nowe united) shoulde hereafter discend to diverse heires of bothe nations (which God forbid): that oathe doeth bind us to assiste anie such successor to our uttermost power, and also to the allegeance of suche a successor of Scotland, contrarie to the loyaltie of such a true Englishe subjecte, bycawse theis wordes are wantinge in the second clause of that oath: his heires and lawfull successors kinges and queenes of this realme.

3. The Pope, beinge a temporall kinge, hath diverse dukes and princes his subjectes, which hold of him their temporall estate, whome (if they deme him his right) he maie lawfullie commaund to be invaded, deposed and killed either by lawe of armes or course of justice. How then can that oathe be taken without manifest perjurie, comprehendinge the negative universallie in the third clause, videlicet: that princes which be excommunicate etc., without anie excepcion?

4. Diverse partes of that oathe doe conteyne pointes of doctrine and schoole learninge controverted amongst the greatest divines both auncient and moderne, as appeareth by the late booke set out of Mr Blackwell's examynacion. Howe then maie anie man – especiallye unlearned – safely sweare that thinge to be true which is doubtfull and questionable, or sweare that he is resolved in conscience, when the thinge he doth sweare unto is in question and not defyned? For allbeit, by the cannon lawe and judgement of all schoole dyvines, it be concluded that the Pope, albeit hee bee an absolute kinge and pastor of the universall Churche, yet yf he fall into heresie maie be deposed, or rather, ipso facto is deposed, yet with safty of conscyence yt cannot be sworne unto, mucheles a question of schoole learnynge untermined; for that in an oathe wee call the sacred majestie of God to witnes, who is truthe it selfe, and therefore ought to sweare nothinge but that wee know assuredlie to be true as that wee lyve.

5. How can a man truelie sweare that he doeth adjure a posicion which he never held, and that the said doctrine is hereticall: yt

being never for such condempned either by aucthoritie of the Churche's auncient fathers, generall counsell or schoole of devines, especiallie seeinge the whole oathe is to be taken accordinge to the expresse wordes and common sence thereof?

6. Finallie, the oathe beinge tendred under great penaltie to the refuser, how can anie man truelie sweare that he doeth take yt hartelie and willinglie?

Printed in Anthony Petti (ed.), *Recusant Documents*, Catholic Record Society, 1968, pp. 160–1

document 14
Lord William Howard

In counties such as Cumberland and Westmorland the great landowners still exercised great influence in the early seventeenth century. Though this report may be exaggerated in places, Lord William obviously used his position to protect catholicism and make life difficult for the Established Church.

In Christenmas last at Bamptom in Westmorland within the diocese of Carlile, the tenantes and servants of my Lord Willyam, together with others in the parish, did erect a Christenmas lord, and did most grosselie disturbe the minister in time of Divine service; the minister himselfe granting toleration because he doth ordinarilie dine and suppe at the Lord Willyam's table, but never prayes with him, and thes Christenmas misrule men some of them drunke to the minister when he was at prayers, others stept into the pulpit and called the parishioners to an offering for mayntenance of ther sport, others of the Lord Willyam's servants came into the Church disguised, others shotte gunnes in the Church, and brought in flagges and banners, others sported themselfes with pies and puddings in the Church, using them as bowles in the Church-allies, others played with dogges, and used them as they used to fear* sheap, and all these were done in the Church and in time of Divine service, and the said Lord doth bring the ministers about him in contempt, scorne and derision.

A minister in London hath confidentlie reported that the said Lord Willyam hath 50,000^{li}. of the Jesuites' moneyes committed into his handes in trust to be disposed for the benefitte of the Jesuites and mayntenance of others of that profession, and for the confirmation of this report Mrs Paine, dwelling in Iselington, did

---

* *To alarm* or *terrify*, the verb *fear* being here employed in an active sense.

tell a gentleman living in Saint Martin's that she had seane a letter written to Doctor Frier, a phisition and recusant, from his daughter, now in a monasterie beyond the seas, wherein she did intreat her father to give thanks to the Lord Willyam for her quarteridge, which she receyved from the Lord Willyam, and she sayd Mrs Payne did see the said letter and hard it read by the Doctor.

The Lord Willyam is thought to keep a priest in his howse, which upon examination may more plainelie be knowne.

The Lord Willyam oppresseth and terrifieth all men with suites (against whom he hath anie show of occasion, though never so triviall) that are not wholie his, and of his faction, in all his Juries and other unfitte courses, as namelie these gentlemen of place and account in the countrie, viz; – Sir James Bellingham, Knight, Sir Henrie Curwen, Knight, Henrie Dacres, Esquire, Richard Rigge, Esquire, Thomas Salkeld, Esquire, in manie severall actions, Hugh Salkeld, gentleman, his owne tenants of Gillesland.

Generallie, if ther be anie suite in the countrie, if he be not a principall mover of it, yet he interposeth and joynes himselfe with the one side though it do nothing at all concerne him, and he so forceth it with his great powre in Court and countrey that all turbulent persons ar by him protected and set on worke. He maintained suites against thes, viz: – Henrie Dacres for hunting, pursued by Edward Harrison by his procurement; Hugh Salkeld, by John Milner; Dorithie Brathwaite, by Thomas her sonne; Sir Edward Musgrave, by Winefride Musgrave and Thomas Wharton; John Flemming, by Robert Sandes: and his interposition betwixt the Earles of Dorsett and Cumberland, ayming at the Sherifwick of Westmorland, as is feared mayntaines the differences betwixt them.

The Lord Willyam doth crosse and oppose the proceedings of the Justices of peace in Westmorland (wher he hath not yet such powre as in Cumberland), and forceth therin suites for ther levies for Bridges, Inmates, Souldiers, etc., to please the people and to become popular, and maketh his tenants the presidents to refuse payments, and of late, at the last Sessions in Westmorland, the constable within the parish of Bampton being pressed by some of the Justices of the peace to present upon oathe what Recusants were in his parish, wher the Lord and his famlie lived, the constable made oathe ther was none.

To mayntaine this his course he plotteth for a sheriffe of his faction for all occurrents that may happen in the countrye, and he entreth bond for him and sendeth downe his patent to engage him.

By thes meanes he maketh law, which is the refuge from oppression, his sword of oppression, and yet if the law may have course to convict him as a recusant the King shall have 2 partes of his landes, and he shall be disabled to serv, which if he be not, all men in those countries for ther owne safetie must and will yeald unto him, for some simple men in that countrie neglecting God for him have given this for a reason, that 'ther is mercie with God but no mercie with my Lord Willyam'.

Mr Ratcliffe hath sent over into a religious house beyond sea 2 of his daughters, wher they yet live.

George Mounsey, a principall dependent of the Lord Willyam and servant to the Countesse of Arrundell at Graistocke in Cumberland, hath divers children which never receyved publique Baptisme, nor himselfe ever convented before authoritie for the same.

Indorsed, Concerninge the Lo: William Howard.

From the *Household Books of Lord William Howard of Naworth Castle*, (**7**)

The English mission
document 15

The missionary priests failed to exploit fully the weakness of the Anglican church in the remoter areas of England. But the mission was still attempting to increase its activity in the moorlands of Westmorland as late as 1638–39. One of the attractions of catholicism in such areas appears to have been the reputation of catholic priests for exorcism.

1638–39: Annual letter of the Durham (Northern) Mission (extended to Hexham)
In these years the number of conversions was, respectively, thirty-seven and eighty. The Fathers had entered upon a new mission in the mountains of Westmorland. Several instances of the miraculous powers of the Church's exorcisms are mentioned. One of them was that of a Protestant woman who had suffered much pain and vexation, which was attributed to witchcraft. She had applied for relief to Protestant ministers, but without effect. She now betook herself to one of the Fathers, who, having instructed her and administered the Sacrament of Penance, applied to her the exorcism of the Church, on which she became perfectly freed from her torments.

Thinking herself now safe, the inconstant woman returned to her former heresy, but soon relapsed into a state of hopeless bodily disease.

From Henry Foley SJ (**4**, vol. 3, pp. 122–3)

document 16
The practices of Philip Howard

The pre-Reformation church put more emphasis on fasting than most of the missionary priests. But the tradition of regular fasting and abstinence from meat continued to be practised by the catholic gentry well into the seventeenth century. This document describes the strict fasting routine followed by Lord Philip Howard.

In the year 1588 soon after his second commitment to close prison, he began to fast three days every week, Mondays, Wednesdays and Fridays, and in them [ate] neither flesh nor fish: But finding by experience that his body was not able to endure so much, he altered it in this manner. That his one meal on Mondays was of flesh: on Wednesdays of fish: on Fridays of neither flesh nor fish, and abstaining also from all whitemeats and wine. And this manner he observed constantly both before and after his arraignment (excepting only the Wednesday immediately following it, wherein he did eat some small thing for supper having then some special need thereof) until he was prescribed by his physicians to alter that course, which was not long before his death. Many time he used also the same abstinence upon Thursdays as upon Mondays with only one meal of flesh. And upon some special days he abstained wholly from all kinds of sustenance either meat or drink. These were the vigils of the feasts of Corpus Christi, of the Ascension of our Saviour, of All Saints, as also the eves of the feasts of the Blessed Virgin, to whom he was particularly devout. Yet he carried it in such manner that none ever had any knowledge thereof, excepting one gentleman his servant, from whom I had it, whose help he used therein. For upon those days as soon as his dinner was brought in, the rest both of his own and the Lieutenant's servants being sent out, and the door fast shut, he made him eat and drink the same quantity that himself usually did on other fasting days, which being done, and the door open again, the other servants came in to take away as at other times without ever perceiving any thing at all, by reason they saw his trenchers and napkin folded, and as much meat eaten as on other days.

From P. Caraman (ed.), *The Other Face*, Longman, 1960, p. 169

document 17
Bequest for the Jesuits and other catholic causes

The English missionary priests depended to a large extent for their finance on the bequests of the English catholic laity. But such bequests had to be left in a discreet manner to avoid falling foul of the law. William Blundell relates how his sister did this in a letter written in 1640.

'Emelia Blundell, my unmarried sister, died at my house, Crosby in Lancashire, on 29 of August 1640. Some few days before her death, she made a Will of which she named me the sole Executor, and did give me thereby all her monies, Bonds and other worldly Goods. (This Will was afterwards attested at Chester, and there I suppose it remaineth still recorded.) But after she had done and that the Witnesses were retired, she told me it was her desire that I should send one hundred pounds to Our Lady's of Loreto and give £100 to the Society of Jesus, and several other sums to other charitable uses: so that it was believed . . . that she did prudently disguise her piety by colour of such a will, as knowing well that our laws did not favour such kind of gifts.'

From Margaret Blundell (ed.), *Letters of William Blundell to his Friends 1620–1648*, Longman, 1933, pp. 7–8

document 18
Fear of catholicism

Fear of catholicism grew in the seventeenth century and rumours of papist plots tended to circulate during times of political crisis. By the 1640s, on the eve of the Civil War, and then during the war itself, the belief in papist plots became far more widespread, and fear of catholicism became a potent political factor.

The 16th of *November*, 1641, there was a cruel and wicked plot discovered about the city of *London*, which was intended against some of the chief members of the High Court of Parliament, and brought to light by a religious man. Therefore it was commanded by the House of Commons that great search should be made for the finding out of two Frenchmen, who were supposed to be the chief agents in this wicked design...they intended the murder of many Protestant Lords, with many other gentlemen, such as Mr Pym and the like, and the papists in *Wales* intended to seize into their hands all the strongholds of *Cheshire* and *Lancashire*, with the adjacent parts, And that in that hurly burly and combustion, the plot was laid and contrived that by the papists at the same instance, the City of *London* should have been surprized, and all the Protestants' throats cut.

A Plot against Norwich to burn the City

Upon the 27 day of *November* [1645] there was a great uproar in *Norwich* concerning the Papists arising there, they being intended to burn the whole city without any remorse, two being appointed privily for the same purpose, one to begin at one end of the City, and the second at the other end. The one was discovered being about to set fire to a thatched house, the other he set the house on fire joining to *High Bridge* street, which was burnt to the ground to the great astonishment of the whole City.

From N. Wallington, *Historical Notices of the Reign of Charles I*, Vol. 2, Richard Bentley, 1869, pp. 44–8

document 19

Anti-catholicism in the Short Parliament, 1640

Though Charles I was far from tolerant towards catholics, Pym's speech to the Short Parliament made the telling point that Charles's policy was directed more towards raising revenue than to converting catholics to the Anglican church. Pym links court catholicism and the re-establishment of diplomatic relations with Rome to the Laudian developments within the Anglican church itself. Pym returned to his anti-catholic theme in the Long Parliament where, as already mentioned, anti-catholicism was a major political factor.

The second generall head is of those grievances that concerne Religion, established by the Lawe of God and man.
1. The encouradgm[en]te given to them of the Popish Religion; divers of them might be of themselves I confesse of peaceable disposicions and good natures, but wee must not looke upon them [as] they are in their natures for the planetts of themselves are of a

slowe and temperate motion, weare they not hurried about by the rappid motions of the spheares, and they carryed about by the violence of the *primum mobile*; soe are all these Papists at the Popes command at any tyme, who onely waytes for blood. I may Instance in Hen. 3 and 4 of France, that were both taken away for alloweinge of Protestants. I desire noe newe lawes, nor a rigid execucon of these wee have but onely soe farr forth as may tend to the saftye of his Majestye. 2dly I observe a suspension of those lawes made against the Papists which are not either executed at all, or are onely so farre used as to make a proffitt by them whereas the said lawes were not made for the Kings revenue, but for distinction.

3dly There is an unrestrayned and mutuall communication of o[u]r Counsell with them [such as at Court].

4thly They are encouradged by admittinge them to greate places of trust in the church and commonwealth (I crave pardon for the last slippe of my tongue), but I wish with all my heart that it neither be soe nowe nor at any tyme hereafter.

5thly The employm[en]t of a *Nuncio* from Rome, whose Councell and businesse is to reduce our land to the Pope.

2) The second head of the second Generall is an Applying of us towards a conversion to Rome.

First by the printing and publishing of many ill Popish bookes with priviledg; the publishing and preachinge [of] many Popish poynts in Pulpitts and disputed in schooles in the Universityes and there maynteyned for sownd Doctrine.

2dly The Introduccon of Popish Ceremonyes such I meane not as the Constitucon since the Reformed Religion continued unto us; But we must introduce againe many of the superstitions and infirme ceremonyes of the most decreppid age of Poperye, as the setting up Altars, boweing to them, and the like.

3) Next I shall observe the dayly discouradgement of those that are the best professors of o[u]r Religion, for not doinge something that were against their consciences. The Manner of howse of Commons usually hath been to reconcile men of nice Consciences to their Bpps [Bishops], thereby to hide the weaknesses of others, but this was a meanes [to publish] the disgrace yt may be to all the world, as these good men for the most part feele.

Now Ceremonyes as bowinge at the name of Jesus [and] rising up at *Gloria Patri* are imposed upon the consciences of men and required as dutye and the omission thereof punish without all grownd. And many Ministers likewise without any ground of Lawe questioned

[for not reading] the Booke of Libertyes on the Saboth a booke
which I must needs affirme hath many thinges faultye. And for not
doing of it have beene deprived of their livings, etc. This is a very
greate greivance being ag[ains]t the foundacon of gover[n]m[en]t.

Speech by John Pym to the Short Parliament, April 1640, printed
in 'Proceedings of the Short Parliament', ed. S. Coates, *Camden
Society 4th Series*, vol. 19, 1977

Bibliography

PRIMARY SOURCES

1   *Calendar of State Papers Domestic, Elizabeth I, James I, Charles I, 1558–1642*

2   *Calendar of State Papers Venetian, 1603–1607*

3   *Catholic Record Society, vols 2, 4, and 39*

4   Henry Foley SJ (ed.), *Records of the English Province of the Society of Jesus, 1877–1887*, vols, 1–6

5   *Exchequer Records*, Pipe Rolls, Recusant Rolls and Lord Treasurer's Remembrance Rolls

6   T. F. Gibson (ed.), *Crosby Records*, Chetham Society, 1887

7   *Household Books of Lord William Howard of Naworth Castle*, Surtees Society, LXVIII, 1877.

8   T. G. Law (ed.), *The Archpriest Controversy*, 2 vols, Camden Society, 1896, 1898

9   A. J. Loomie (ed.), *Spain and the Jacobean Catholics*, Catholic Record Society, 64, 1973 and vol. 2, 68, 1978

10   W. Palmes SJ, *Life of Mrs Dorothy Lawson*, ed. G. B. Richardson, 1851

11   A. C. Southern (ed.), *An Elizabethan Recusant Household*, Sands & Co., Glasgow 1954

12   James Spedding (ed.), *The Works of Francis Bacon*, Longman, Green, Longman, and Roberts, vol. XI, 1858–61

13   Lawrence Vaux, *A Catechism of Christian Doctrine*, Chetham Society, 1885

14   *Westminster Archive Manuscripts*

SECONDARY SOURCES

15   Gordon Albion, *Charles I and the Court of Rome*, Burns & Oates, 1935

16   G. Anstruther OP, *Vaux of Harrowden*, R. H. Johns, Newport Mon., 1953

17   G. Anstruther OP, *The Seminary Priests: Elizabeth I 1558–1603*, St Edmunds College, Ware; Urshaw College, Durham, 1968

18   G. Anstruther OP, *The Seminary Priests, vol. 2: Early Stuarts 1603–1659*, Mayhew-McCrimmon, 1975

19   J. C. H. Aveling, *Northern Catholics: the Catholic Recusants of the North Riding of Yorkshire, 1558–1790*, Chapman, 1966

20   J. C. H. Aveling, *The Catholic Recusants of the West Riding of Yorkshire, 1558–1790*, Leeds Philosophical and Literary Society, vol. X, pt VI, 1963

21   J. C. H. Aveling, *The Handle and the Axe*, Blond & Briggs, 1976

22   Bernard Basset, *The English Jesuits*, Burns & Oates, 1967

23   C. G. Bayne, *Anglo-Roman Relations 1558–1565*, Clarendon Press, 1913

24   John Bossy, *The English Catholic Community 1570–1850*, Darton, Longman & Todd, 1975

25   Philip Caraman, *Henry Garnet, 1555–1606 and the Gunpowder Plot*, Longmans, 1964

26   C. H. Carter, *The Secret Diplomacy of the Habsburgs*, Columbia University Press, New York and London, 1964

27   T. H. Clancy, *Papist Pamphleteers*, Loyola University Press, Chicago, 1964

28   J. T. Cliffe, *The Yorkshire Gentry from the Reformation to the Civil War*, Athlone Press, 1969

29   Claire Cross, *The Royal Supremacy in the Elizabethan Church*, Allen & Unwin, 1969

30   A. G. Dickens, *The English Reformation*, Fontana/Collins, 1967

31   A. G. Dickens, *Lollards and Protestants in the Diocese of York, 1509–1558*, Oxford University Press, 1959

32   F. C. Dietz, *English Public Finance, 1558–1641*, Century, New York, 1943

33   Francis Edwards SJ, *Guy Fawkes: The Real Story of the Gunpowder Plot*, Burns & Oates, 1969

34   G. R. Elton, *Reform and Reformation, England 1509–1558*, Edward Arnold, 1979 reprint

35   H. O. Evennett, *The Spirit of the Counter Reformation*, University of Notre Dame Press, 1968

36   A. Fletcher, *Tudor Rebellions*, Longman, 2nd edn 1973

37   S. R. Gardiner, *History of England 1603–42*, Longman, Green, 1883–84

38   W. Haller, *Foxe's Book of Martyrs and the Elect Nation*, Jonathan Cape, 1963

39   William P. Hauguard, *Elizabeth and the English Reformation*, Cambridge University Press, 1968

40 C. Haigh, *Reformation and Resistance in Tudor Lancashire*, Cambridge University Press, 1975

41 M. J. Havran, *The Catholics in Caroline England*, Oxford University Press, 1962

42 M. J. Havran, *Caroline Courtier: The Life of Lord Cottington*, Macmillan, 1973

43 F. Heal and R. O'Day, *Church and Society in England, Henry VIII to James I*, Macmillan, 1977

44 Philip Hughes, *The Reformation in England*, Burns & Oates, 1963 reprint

45 Philip Hughes, *Rome and the Counter Reformation*, Burns & Oates, 1942

46 G. Huxley, *Life of Endymion Porter*, Chatto & Windus, 1959

47 W. K. Jordan, *The Development of Religious Toleration in England*, vol. 2, Allen & Unwin, 1936

48 M. D. R. Leys, *Catholics in England 1559–1829: A Social History*, Longmans, 1961

49 Wallace MacCaffrey, *The Shaping of the Elizabethan Regime*, Princeton University Press, 1968

50 P. McGrath, *Papists and Puritans under Elizabeth I*, Batsford, 1967

51 B. Magee, *The English Recusants*, Burns & Oates, 1938

52 R. B. Manning, *Religion and Society in Elizabethan Sussex*, Leicester University Press, 1969

53 David Mathew, *Catholicism in England, The Portrait of a Minority: its Culture and Tradition*, Eyre & Spottiswoode, 3rd edn, 1955

54 David Mathew, *The Jacobean Age*, Longmans, Greene Co. Ltd., 1938

55 A. O. Meyer, *England and the Catholic Church under Queen Elizabeth*, Routledge & Kegan Paul, 1967 reprint

56 J. L. Miller, *Popery and Politics in England 1660–1688*, Cambridge University Press, 1973

57 J. E. Neale, *Elizabeth I and Her Parliaments 1558–1581, 1581–1603*, 2 vols, Cape, 1953, 1957

58 Carola Oman, *Henrietta Maria*, White Lion Publishers, 1936

59 J. H. Pollen, *The English Catholics in the Reign of Queen Elizabeth*, Longmans, Greene Co., 1920

60 A. Pritchard, *Catholic Loyalism in Elizabethan England*, Scolar University Press, 1938

61 Conrad Russell, *The Crisis of Parliaments: English History 1509–1660*, Oxford University Press, 1971

62 A. Hassell Smith, *Country and Court: Government and Politics in Norfolk 1558–1603*, Clarendon Press, 1974

63 Lawrence Stone, *Crisis of the Aristocracy*, Clarendon Press, 1965

64 M. A. Tierney (ed.), [Charles] Dodd's *Church History of England*, Charles Dolman, 5 vols, 1839–43

65 K. Thomas, *Religion and the Decline of Magic*, Penguin, 1973

66 W. J. R. Trimble, *The Elizabethan Catholic Laity*, Harvard University Press, 1964

67 Joan Wake, *The Brudenells of Deene*, Cassell & Co., 1954

68 D. H. Willson, *King James VI and I*, Cape, 1966 reprint

69 P. Zagorin, *Court and Country: the Beginning of the English Revolution*, Routledge & Kegan Paul, 1969

ARTICLES

70 J. C. H. Aveling, 'Post Reformation Catholicism in East Yorkshire', East Yorkshire Local History Society, 1960

71 J. C. H. Aveling, 'Some Aspects of Yorkshire Catholic Recusant History: 1558–1791', *Studies in Church History*, IV, ed. G. J. Cummings, Leiden, 1967

72 R. I. Bladley, 'Blacko and the Counter Reformation' in *From Renaissance to Counter Reformation*, ed. C. H. Carter, 1964.

73 John Bossy, 'Rome and the English Catholics: a Question of Geography', *Historical Journal*, VII, no. 1, 1964

74 John Bossy, 'English Catholics and the French Marriage, 1577–81', *Recusant History*, vol. 5, no. 1, 1959

75 John Bossy, 'Henry IV, the Appellants and the Jesuits', *Recusant History*, vol. 8, no. 2, 1965

76 John Bossy, 'The Character of Elizabethan Catholicism' in *Crisis in Europe 1560–1660*, ed. T. Aston, Routledge & Kegan Paul, 1965

77 John Bossy, 'The English Catholic Community 1603–1625', in *The Reign of James VI and I*, ed. A. G. R. Smith, Macmillan, 1973

78 B. Capp, 'Godly Rule and English Millenarianism', *Past and Present*, no. 52, August 1971

79 T. M. Clancy, 'English Catholics and the Papal Deposing Power', *Recusant History* pt I, vol. 6, no. 3, 1961–62; pt II, vol. 6, no. 5, 1961–62; pt III, vol. 7, no. 1, 1963

80 R. Clifton, 'Popular Fear of Catholicism during the English Civil War', *Past and Present*, no. 52, 1971

81 R. Clifton, 'Fear of Popery', in *The Origins of the English Civil War*, ed. C. Russell, Macmillan, 1975

82   A. G. Dickens, 'The First Stages of Romanist Recusancy, 1560–1590', *Yorkshire Archaeological Journal*, XXXV, 1943

83   A. G. Dickens, 'The Extent and Character of Recusancy in Yorkshire in 1604', *Yorkshire Archaeological Journal*, XXXVII, 1948

84   A. H. Dodd, 'The Spanish Treason, the Gunpowder Plot and the Catholic Refugees', *English Historical Review*, LIII, 1938

85   J. A. Hilton, 'Recusancy in Elizabethan Durham', *Recusant History*, vol. 14, no. 1, 1977

86   J. S. Leatherbarrow, 'Lancashire Elizabethan Recusants', Chetham Society, vol. 110, 1947

87   K. J. Lindley, 'The Lay Catholics of England in the Reign of Charles I', *Journal of Ecclesiastical History*, XXII, 1971

88   K. J. Lindley, 'The Part Played by Catholics', in *Religion, Politics and the English Civil War*, ed. Brian Manning, Edward Arnold, 1973

89   A. J. Loomie SJ, 'Toleration and Diplomacy: the Religious Issue in Anglo-Spanish Relations 1603–5', *Transactions of the American Philosophical Society*, LIII, part 6, 1963

90   A. J. Loomie SJ, 'Guy Fawkes in Spain, the "Spanish Treason" in Spanish Documents', Special Supplement of *Bulletin of the Institute of Historical Research*, Nov. 1971

91   G. Mattingley, 'William Allen and Catholic Propaganda in England', *Travaux d'Humanism et Renaissance*, XXVIII, 1957

92   A. O. Meyer, 'Charles I and Rome', *English Historical Review*, 1913

93   P. R. Newman, 'Catholic Royalist Activists in the North 1642–1646', *Recusant History*, 14, no. 1, 1977

94   G. Sitwell, 'Leander Jones's Mission to England', *Recusant History*, 5, no. 4, 1960

95   P. W. Thomas, 'Two Cultures? Court and Country under Charles I', in *The Origins of the English Civil War*, ed. C. Russell, Macmillan, 1975

96   N. Tyacke, 'Puritanism, Arminianism and Counter Revolution' in *The Origins of the English Civil War*, ed. C. Russell, Macmillan, 1975

97   K. R. Wark, 'Elizabethan Recusancy in Cheshire', Chetham Society, 1971

98   Carol Z. Wiener, 'The Beleaguered Isle', *Past and Present*, 51, 1971

THESES

99 A. Davidson, 'Roman Catholicism in Oxfordshire from the late Elizabethan Period to the Civil War', Bristol PhD thesis, 1970

100 M. O'Dwyer, 'Catholic Recusants in Essex *c.* 1580–*c.* 1600', London MA thesis, 1960

101 F. X. Walker, 'The Implementation of the Elizabethan Statutes against Recusants', London PhD thesis, 1961

ADDITIONS

102 G. R. Elton, 'Parliament in the Sixteenth Century: Functions and Fortunes', *Historical Journal*, 22, 2, 1979

103 I. D. Grosvenor, 'Catholics and Politics: The Worcestshire Election of 1604', *Recusant History*, 14, no. 13, May 1976

104 C. Haigh, 'The Fall of a Church or the Rise of a Sect? Post Reformation Catholicism in England', review article in *Historical Journal*, 21, 1, 1978

105 C. Haigh, 'The Continuity of Catholicism in the English Reformation', *Past and Present*, 93, 1981

106 C. Haigh, 'From Monopoly to Minority: Catholicism in Tudor England', *Transactions of the Royal Historical Society*, Fifth series, 31, 1981

107 N. L. Jones, 'Profiting from Religious Reform: the land rush of 1559', *Historical Journal*, 22, 2, 1979

108 A. J. Fletcher, *The Outbreak of the English Civil War*, Arnold, 1981

Index